DANIEL
WHAT GOD CAN DO
STAFFORD NORTH

21st Century Christian Publishing

ISBN: 978-0-89098-922-7

©2016 by 21st Century Christian

2809 12th Ave S, Nashville, TN 37204

All rights reserved.

All rights reserved. No part of this publication may be reproduced, stored in a retrieval system, or transmitted in any form or by any means—electronic, mechanical, photocopy, recording, digital, or otherwise—without the written permission of the publisher.

Unless otherwise noted Scripture quotations are from the New International Version.

Scripture quotations taken from THE HOLY BIBLE, NEW INTERNATIONAL VERSION®, NIV®

Copyright © 1973, 1978, 1984, 2011 by Biblica, Inc.™

Used by permission. All rights reserved worldwide.

Cover design by Jonathan Edelhuber

TABLE OF CONTENTS

PREFACE
Daniel: What God Can Do 5

To the Teacher 9

Chronology for the Study of Daniel 13

CHAPTER 1
Faithful Under Hardship 15

CHAPTER 2
God Works Through a Dream 25

CHAPTER 3
Decision in the Plain of Dura 37

CHAPTER 4
The Mighty Has Fallen 45

CHAPTER 5
God Sends a Mysterious Message 53

CHAPTER 6
Faithfulness, Persecution, and Deliverance 61

CHAPTER 7
Four Beasts and a Son of Man 71

CHAPTER 8
The Ram and the Goat and the Future 85

CHAPTER 9
Seventy Sevens and the Coming Messiah 95

CHAPTER 10
Daniel and Angels 109

CHAPTER 11
The Most Detailed Prophecy in the Bible 117

CHAPTER 12
The Prophecy Comes to a "Time of the End" 127

Completed Charts 141

Appendix 147

Study Guide 155

Bibliography 167

PREFACE

Daniel: What God Can Do

Stuart Hamblen was an actor in westerns and a radio show host in the 1940s. His life-style included drinking and other bad behavior. After attending an early Billy Graham revival, Hamblen decided to believe in Jesus and to change his life. At a party one night, actor John Wayne asked Hamblen if it had been hard to change his life. Hamblen replied, "It is no secret what God can do." Wayne told him he should write a song about that. That very night, Hamblen went home and within a few hours had written the hymn, "It is no secret what God can do; what He's done for others, He'll do for you."

I have used the expression "What God Can Do" in the title of this book about Daniel because I believe there is no greater account in the Old Testament about what God is able to do than in the book of Daniel. Imagine! A teenager is taken captive from his home in Judah to the land of Babylon, about a thousand miles as a caravan would have traveled, eventually to become the second in command in two of the largest and greatest world empires. Additionally, through this man, God revealed His most amazing prophecies about world empires yet to come.

Each chapter in this book about Daniel will move on two tracks. The first will share thoughts about the personal life of Daniel and/or the meaning of the prophecies God revealed through him. This track will also include personal applications in each chapter to encourage and inspire us to follow Daniel's example in our own lives. The second track will be thoughts about sermons (and Bible classes), which a minister can preach from

PREFACE

the book of Daniel to enlighten and encourage his congregation. While the first portion of the chapter will help the preacher tell the story of an event in Daniel's life in an interesting way or describe the prophecy in the chapter, the second part will provide more specific thoughts and brief outlines of sermons he could preach.

The Appendix has information on two topics: (1) the history of the world from the time of Daniel to the time of Christ and (2) a discussion of when the book of Daniel was written. If you are teaching the book of Daniel, you will want to establish for your class the time of its writing. Some claim that Daniel was written after the events which he claims to foretell. If that is true, the book is a fraud. Our examination should prove otherwise.

In 1975, I began delivering a set of lessons on the book of Revelation which I have given, in one form or another, nearly 300 times. In 2003, I put these lessons in written form in a book called *Unlocking Revelation* (21st Century Christian), which has had a rather wide circulation. Though my study of Daniel has not gone back that far, I have taught it in classes at Oklahoma Christian University and brought lessons on it in many places. So, now, I have decided to provide a book on Daniel as a companion piece to the book on Revelation.

The first six chapters of Daniel tell of his being carried to Babylon, of his training in the culture and language of that country, and describe his personal life and service to the kings of Babylon and Persia. Chapters 7 through 12 contain prophecies God gave Daniel to share and to be preserved so that those who saw the fulfillment of the prophecies in later centuries could understand that God, through His prophets, could make specific and detailed predictions of the future. Though there are sometimes differing opinions about the meaning of the prophecies, I will share the conclusion I have reached through my study of many scholars to explain the meaning of these prophecies. By studying these predictions, we will build faith in the ability of the Bible's authors to predict the future accurately and will see in these prophecies a foundation for the coming of Jesus.

This book, then, has four functions: to give the meaning of the content of the book of Daniel; to help us make personal applications from the book to our own lives; to provide ideas from Daniel for developing sermons; to provide information in the final section for teaching a thirteen-week class on the book of Daniel.

Let us embark, then, on an exciting journey that begins more than 2,500 years ago in the small country of Judah, just along the western shore of the Mediterranean Sea. What is going to happen to the people of that small country? What will happen to their major city, Jerusalem? What is all of this going to say about their God as He is compared with the gods of other nations around them?

Just remember, "It is no secret what God can do!"

To the Teacher

Congratulations if you are planning to teach Daniel! The book is both instructional and inspirational. God took delight in teaching us by stories about people who have pleased Him, and Daniel ranks high among those God has used both for His purposes and for our benefit.

At the end of this book, there are teaching suggestions for thirteen lessons on the book of Daniel. Since there are twelve chapters in Daniel, these almost match lesson to chapter. Before beginning the class, you should give thought to the objectives below. Students are much more likely to learn if they know what they are supposed to be able to do by the time the class is over. Otherwise, you are playing basketball with no goals. So, here are eight objectives for you and your students to achieve together.

1. The student can relate the historical circumstances surrounding the story of Daniel, including what was happening in the kingdom of Judah and in other kingdoms related to the story.

2. The student can provide a date for key events in the story of Daniel.

3. The student can give five reasons why we can believe that the Daniel of the story actually wrote the book, thus indicating that the book contains accurate predictions of the future.

4. The student can tell the basic story related to the life of Daniel as given in the first six chapters of Daniel.

TO THE TEACHER

5. The student can draw from memory the chart summarizing the five prophecies of Daniel.
6. The student can describe the qualities of God as shown in the book of Daniel.
7. The student can explain that Daniel and his prophecies reveal how God was working out His plan to save people from sin.
8. The student can make practical applications from the story of Daniel to his own life, having recorded them on a sheet provided in his notebook.

As you teach the class, try to involve the students as much as possible through using the question and answer or the group discussion method. If you have a large class making these activities impractical, still give opportunities for student participation, particularly in the practical applications. Provide the student a loose-leaf notebook in which to keep sheets that you hand out with various class periods and in which to keep notes he may take during the lessons.

If you wish to go a step further, develop worksheets students can complete during each lesson. Then tell them to study these worksheets as reminders of what you have studied and give them a review quiz (not a test because that sounds threatening) at the start of class each time. Thus they learn from what you say, what you post on the board or screen, what they write down, and what they review. This repetition of the basic content will help them to remember it. If you want to save time in class, put the review quiz sheets on a chair or table so the students can pick them up and write in their answers before the actual class time starts. Then at the first of the class, you can quickly give the answers as a review from the previous class. This review will be good even for those who choose not to do the review sheet because they can fill it in as a review for themselves.

Should you wish a fuller set of teaching materials to use with the course or want additional reference material, go to *www.eBibleStudy.org* and click on the Daniel lessons. There you will find worksheets and quizzes on the book of Daniel. You may need to adapt these, depending on how you are teaching the classes. I wrote these materials, and they are free through the College of Biblical Studies at Oklahoma Christian University.

Be sure to use the charts to help the students have an easy way to put together the prophecies in Daniel. Although it should not be your goal for the student to remember all the details of the prophecies, it should be your goal that they can complete from memory the final chart, which lets them summarize the kingdoms and the prophecies about them.

One of the major shortcomings of most adult classes is that there is little or no practical application of the lessons. Be sure, therefore, that you allow sufficient time for application. You will do well to let students help with making the applications. Ask them, "How can you use this lesson at work, at school, in your family, at church, when you drive, with your neighbors?" Then be sure to push the discussion until the application becomes specific.

Study well to prepare, and work hard to be clear, to be specific about the objectives the students should reach, to involve the students in learning, to use good repetition, and to allow for good application. May God bless your teaching.

~ Stafford North

Chronology for the Study of Daniel

(*Some dates approximate*)

722 BC   The Kingdom of Israel (Northern Kingdom) falls to Assyria, and Israelites are scattered throughout other nations never to return.

626 BC   Jeremiah prophesies that Nebuchadnezzar of Babylon will conquer the Kingdom of Judah, destroy their cities and that the people will remain in captivity for seventy years (Jeremiah 25:8-11).

612 BC   The rising kingdom of Babylon conquers Nineveh and becomes the dominant power in the world.

605 BC   Nebuchadnezzar comes against Jerusalem and conquers it. He takes some captive to Babylon, including Daniel and three other young men. He puts them in training to be part of his council of advisors. He also takes some vessels from the temple to put in the storehouse of his idols (Daniel 1).

605 BC   Nebuchadnezzar becomes king in Babylon after the death of his father, Nebopolassar.

603 BC   Nebuchadnezzar has a dream that Daniel interprets (Daniel 2).

602 BC   Jewish king Jehoikim rebels against Babylonian authority.

597 BC   King Nebuchadnezzar conquers Jerusalem a second time and takes more captives, including Ezekiel, who lives with the Jewish captives in Babylon and prophesies to encourage them.

CHRONOLOGY FOR THE STUDY OF DANIEL

589 BC Daniel's three friends refuse to bow before an idol (Daniel 3).

586 BC Jewish king Zedekiah rebels and the Babylonians come a third time and destroys Jerusalem along with the temple Solomon had built. Many more captives are taken to Babylon.

562 BC Nebuchadnezzar dies.

555 BC Nabonidus, with his son, Belshazzar, reign over Babylon (Daniel 5, 7 and 8).

539 BC The handwriting on the wall appears to Belshazzar, and the Persians under Cyrus conquer Babylon (Daniel 5; Isaiah 45:1ff).

538 BC Daniel receives the vision about the seventy sevens (Daniel 9).

538 BC Cyrus allows 42,360 Jews to return to Judah (Ezra 1:1-4; Daniel 10-12).

530 BC Daniel dies in Babylon.

CHAPTER 1

Faithful Under Hardship

In 605 BC, Nebuchadnezzar of Babylon led his army to Jerusalem, the capital city of the nation of Judah, located on the southeastern edge of the Mediterranean Sea. He had just defeated the Assyrian and Egyptian alliance at the battle of Carchemish and was pushing westward. That brought him to lay siege against Jerusalem and, of course, the small and weak Judeans were no match for the greatest power in the world, so they surrendered.

The coming of the Babylonians against the Jews had been predicted for many years. Isaiah 39:5, written more than a hundred years in advance and Jeremiah 25, written a few years before, told the Jews that because of their failure to obey God, they would be punished with captivity. Moses, in Deuteronomy 28:49ff, had told the people that if they were unfaithful to God, the outcome would be captivity to a nation from far away whose language they did not know.

Nebuchadnezzar did not wish to destroy Jerusalem, and so he left Jehoiakim as king over Judah. He did take back to Babylon some of the utensils used in the Jewish temple worship so that he could put them in the treasure house of his god. We are not told what these utensils were but they do appear again in Daniel 5 when they are used for drinking at a pagan feast.

Nebuchadnezzar also decided to take back with him to Babylon some of the best young men from noble families of Judah. He found those with no physical defect, who were handsome, who demonstrated they were smart by showing aptitude in every kind of learning, and who were quick to understand. He wanted these

FAITHFUL UNDER HARDSHIP

young men to serve him in governing Babylon.

Among the young men taken captive were Daniel, Hanniah, Mishael, and Azariah. Imagine yourself in their position. Since we know that Daniel lived to around 530 BC, seventy-five years later, these boys were likely no older than mid-teens. They were taken away from family, away from friends, away from teachers, away from all who follow the same God they do, away from their customs of dress, and even away from those who spoke their language. And there was no means of communication once they were gone. Culture shock of the greatest magnitude!

What was to happen to these four young men? They were put into a three-year training program in the king's palace to study the language and literature of the Babylonians. King Nebuchadnezzar wanted some among his officials who could help him know about countries he has conquered and who could serve among his officials to help him oversee all the land he had conquered.

These young men had fine quarters in which to live, had the best instructors, ate the best food, and had excellent protection. They were not to be mistreated in any way even though they were from a conquered people and were hundreds of miles away from their original home.

Well, someone might think, *That sounds pretty good. Great lodging, great teachers, great food, and at the seat of the greatest power in the world. And they had to pay no tuition at "Nebuchadnezzar University."*

But wait!!! Some complications began to arise. They were given new names, names which include a reference to the pagan gods of their new nation. And, on top of that, the food they were given would "defile" them (1:8) because in some way it did not fit the requirements of food which Jews were to eat under the Law of Moses. Either the food was not prepared as the Law required or had been offered before idols. Either of these circumstances would make it wrong for them to eat if they wished to keep the

Daniel: What God Can Do

Jewish Law while living in a new land.

So, imagine yourself in that situation. Although the God of the Jews had not kept them from being captured, the situation had not turned out too badly for them. In the new place, however, no one cared about the Law of Moses or trying to live by those standards. In addition, refusing to do as they are told could mean they would be killed. What shall they do?

They have several options. (1) They can decide that since they are in a totally new situation where no one knows about their God, they will just drop the matter and do the popular thing. (2) They can tell God they don't want to violate His teachings, but that they are sure He would allow them a waiver under these difficult circumstances. (3) They can appeal for some change in the food but, if that is not accepted, then they will give in rather than to make a big deal about the matter—at least they will have tried. Or (4) they can take a stand and refuse under any circumstances to eat food that will defile themselves.

So what will they do? "But Daniel resolved not to defile himself with the royal food and wine, and he asked the chief official for permission not to defile himself this way" (1:8). The official told Daniel that he was afraid not to do exactly as the king had commanded about the food because it might mean "his head," so he refused their request.

But Daniel had "resolved," so he did not give in. He next went to a different person, the one who actually served them the food, and asked that he and his friends be given a test about the food. Give them vegetables and water for ten days and then see how they compared with those who had been eating the royal food. This person agreed and at the end of the ten days, he concluded that they looked healthier and better nourished than those eating from the king's table. So he continued to give them that food. Daniel's determination had paid off, and God was blessing him.

Let's imagine a similar situation today. A Christian young woman has great singing talent and is offered an opportunity to sing in an off-Broadway show in New York City. She thinks the opportunity is too good to pass up, so she goes, but then finds herself in the midst of a totally different culture. Although the language is still English, people use words she has always avoided. None of those with her ever goes to church or even speaks of anything religious. She wants to succeed, but fears that if she does not go along, she will not advance in her career. What shall she do? Shall she (1) not jeopardize this wonderful opportunity by going against the flow or (2) go along a little bit and not let anyone know about her previous convictions or (3) shall she stand by her convictions and succeed on her terms or change her aspirations?

Let's take another scenario. Suppose a high school graduate needs a job and finds an opening working on an oil crew. The pay is good and the work is honest, but the people around him not only are not religious, but their actions are totally different from what he has learned at church. They get drunk, use foul language, gamble, and engage in sexual activity outside of marriage. He is going to stick out like a sore thumb if he does only what he has been taught is right. He would not, of course, go along with them completely, but maybe he might just do enough with them so they would not make fun of him. He will not keep this job forever and next time he can get a job that lets him go back to what he has believed. Wouldn't that be okay?

Such situations could be multiplied: a teenage girl who wants to make close friends among those who do not share her faith, a young man who goes to college and finds himself in a dormitory where the party scene is a big deal, a high school student who gets involved in sports activities and finds that those on the team engage in things that are sinful, a man whose job involves lots of travel and finds himself tempted to get involved in sinful activities. After all, who will know?

Eventually, nearly everyone will find himself in a situation that will call for a decision like Daniel's. His example tells us exactly what to do. Resolve!!! Resolve to stay with what the Bible teaches us to do, to stay with the example Daniel has given us, to continue with what we have been taught at church and by Christian people. Daniel was tactful. Daniel was persistent. Daniel was firm. Daniel stayed true to his convictions.

Now for the rest of the story. Daniel and his friends completed their three-year course of instruction and excelled. "To these four young men God gave knowledge and understanding of all kinds of literature and learning" (1:17). The king himself gave the final oral exam and found that no one was their equal. "In every matter of wisdom and understanding about which the king questioned them, he found them ten times better than all the magicians and enchanters in his whole kingdom" (1:20).

Their faithfulness led to great success.

Note two or three other things about the story. First, the role of God. In verse 2, we are told that God delivered Jehoiakim king of Judah into Nebuchadnezzar's hand. Verse 9 says that God caused the official to show favor and sympathy to Daniel. And verse 17 says that God gave knowledge and understanding to Daniel, Hananiah, Mishael, and Azariah. God moves in mysterious ways His wonders to perform. Throughout this book, we note that "it is no secret what God can do." In this first chapter alone, we learn that God kept His promise that if the Jews kept on wandering away after idols, He would send them away in captivity under the Babylonians, and He used Nebuchadnezzar to carry out His will. God also wanted Daniel and his friends to be His representatives in a heathen court, as we shall soon see, so He protected them, got them favorable treatment, and helped them with their studies.

Just how should we expect help from God today? First, we cannot know how God is working behind the scenes. How many times have we heard people say that something in their lives they thought would be a great setback turned out to be a blessing? We know that for God's people He does work. So many verses in the Bible tell us that God cares for His people. First Peter 5:7, for example, encourages us to cast all our anxiety on God who cares for us.

Second, God does not cause everything that happens to us. Many things happen to us because of a decision someone else makes and that decision impacts us, like a drunk driver or a person on a shooting rampage or an unscrupulous business partner. Likewise, sometimes things happen, both good and bad, because of decisions we make ourselves. There is a way, however, in which any situation can work for our good if we will let God work in our lives (Romans 8:28).

Third, as it was in the case of Daniel, the ultimate outcome for God's people will be good. This does not mean that every piece of the puzzle will be as we would like it or that the script will always be as we would have written it, but at the end, if we are faithful, the outcome will be good. Unfortunately, too many have something happen along the way that is not what they had hoped, so they turn their backs on God. They do not get the job they wanted, they lose the girlfriend they wanted, they have an accident or illness, someone mistreats them even when they did the right thing, they lose a loved one when many prayed for her. Daniel and his friends did get carried far from home away from all they loved, but God worked with them in that situation for good things to happen for Him and for them.

So, the story of Daniel, Hananiah, Mishael, and Azariah is useful for us. Their example teaches us to resolve to do right in every situation and to depend on God to help work things for an eventual good outcome.

Sermon Thoughts from Daniel 1

What God Can Do: He Works Among Nations

In Acts 17:26, when Paul spoke to the Athenians about the God unknown to them, he said that God "determined the time set for them and the exact places where they should live." God does care about what goes on in His world. Though He allows people and nations to make their own choices and to receive the good or bad consequences of those choices, God, nonetheless, is able to use the outcome of their choices within His own plan. Peter on Pentecost, for example, speaks on an individual level when he says that the Jews, with the help of wicked men, put Jesus to death but that their action was part of God's set purpose and foreknowledge. God took what they did that was wrong and used it as part of His plan.

1. **God warns nations that immorality will doom the nation.** When Israel is about to enter the Promised Land, God tells them that if they go after idols and disobey other commands, they will be cast out of the land (Deuteronomy 28:64). Solomon wrote that, "Righteousness exalts a nation, but sin condemns any people (Proverbs 14:34).

2. **God brings down nations that practice immorality.** Think of the flood, Sodom and Gomorrah, and the Israelites during the time of the Judges when, time after time, God punished the Israelites because of their idolatry and other evil deeds. And the Babylonian Captivity. A great book on this subject is *When Nations Die* by Jim Nelson Black.

3. **God exalts nations that practice righteousness.** In Deuteronomy 30, Moses outlines the good that will come to Israel when they obey God.

What God Can Do
Tell the story of Daniel 1. (Narration)
From the story we learn that—(Application)

1. **Obedience to God will be rewarded.** (See Isaiah 40:30-31). Daniel and his friends were blessed during their three years of training because they were faithful to God's commands. Joseph did not find immediate reward for being obedient, but he did eventually. Our obedience will also be rewarded.

2. **Obedience to God is often the path to promotion.** Daniel and Joseph are both examples of men who obeyed God in their youth and who were elevated to high positions. Though not always the case, it is often true that honesty and love for your neighbor in business endeavors will sometimes bring higher positions.

3. **Obedience to God often leads to achievement of His purposes.** While Daniel and Joseph didn't know at the time that they were playing a role which would enable God to achieve His purposes and to help His people, their faithfulness allowed God to use them for that purpose. God can use us today to achieve His purposes when we are true to His Word.

Plan to Do Right

1. **Daniel had convictions.** So how can we develop the right convictions?
2. **Daniel had companions.** So how do we develop helpful companions?
3. **Daniel had courage.** So how do we develop the right courage?

The Process for Pleasing God

1. **Decide what is right.** Learn Bible teaching to guide you,
2. **Declare what is right.** Share with others what you will do. Accountability partners.
3. **Do what is right.** When the time comes, live by your convictions.

How Daniel Did What Was Right

Tell the story of Daniel 1 under the headings of: the problem, the request, the result. From this story, conclude that—

Daniel believed in God, regardless of the circumstances.

Daniel obeyed God, regardless of the consequences.

Then tell our story.

> We must believe in God, regardless of the circumstances.
> When we suffer from illness or loss, we must believe that God will find a way to bring us blessings.

We must obey God, regardless of the consequences.

> When it appears that we may suffer bad consequences for doing the right thing, we must still obey God believing that He will make it right.

CHAPTER 2

God Works Through a Dream

One night while Daniel and his friends were still in their training, King Nebuchadnezzar was asleep in his beautiful palace. He awoke in a troubled state of mind because he knew he had experienced a dream. He either could not remember what the dream was or he remembered it but wanted to test his counselors to see if they could tell him what the dream was. He was so concerned about the dream that, still in the middle of the night, he summoned his wise men, magicians, enchanters, sorcerers, and astrologers. When they had assembled, Nebuchadnezzar demanded that they both tell him what he had dreamed and what it meant.

His counselors were shocked that he would ask them to tell him what he dreamed. If he would just tell them the dream, they implored, they could provide ideas for what it might mean. No one, they said, had ever asked others both to tell what a dream was as well as what it meant. King Nebuchadnezzar made it quite clear, however, that he would not be satisfied until they told him both the dream and its meaning. When they again asked him to reveal the dream so they could interpret it, he became quite angry and ordered the execution of all the wise men of Babylon. Even though Daniel, Hananiah, Mishael, and Azariah had not been part of the group summoned before the king, apparently because they had not finished their course of study, they were told that they still would be among those to be executed because of the group's failure to tell the king his dream and its meaning.

When Daniel became aware of the problem, he went to Arioch,

GOD WORKS THROUGH A DREAM

the commander of the king's guard and "spoke to him with wisdom and tact" (2:14). Upon learning all about the situation, Daniel went into the presence of King Nebuchadnezzar and asked for a delay in the executions so that he could reveal the dream. The king, who obviously thought well of Daniel, granted him the extra time.

Then Daniel returned to his living quarters and explained things to his friends and asked them to plead for mercy from the God of heaven so they would not be killed. Having prayed, Daniel then waited for God to answer. During the night, God revealed the mystery to him, telling him both what the dream was and its meaning.

Then Daniel broke forth in prayer, saying "Praise be to the name of God for ever and ever; wisdom and power are his. He changes times and seasons; he deposes kings and raises up others. He gives wisdom to the wise and knowledge to the discerning. . . I thank and praise you, God of my ancestors: You have given me wisdom and power, you have made known to me what we asked of you, you have made known the dream of the king" (2:20-23).

Daniel then went to Arioch and told him not to execute the wise men and asked to be taken to the king, promising to reveal the dream. When Arioch took him to the palace to enter the presence of Nebuchadnezzar, the king asked, "Are you able to tell me what I saw in my dream and interpret it (2:26)? Daniel replied that no wise men or enchanters could do it, but that there was a God in heaven who reveals mysteries and who would make known the dream.

This was, so far as we know, the first time Daniel had been involved in interpreting a dream but, since God had revealed the dream and interpretation to him, he felt confident that he could meet the king's demands. He even told the king that the dream would deal with what would happen in the days to come.

Then Daniel told the king what he had dreamed as God had revealed it. He told the king he had seen an enormous, dazzling statue, awesome in appearance. The head of the statue was of pure gold, its chest and arms of silver, its belly and thighs of bronze, its legs of iron, and its feet of iron mixed with clay. Then the action of the dream began. A rock was cut out, not by human hands, and it came down and struck the statue on its feet of iron and clay and smashed them. With its feet cut out from under it, the statue fell and was broken to pieces and became like chaff on a threshing floor. Then the wind came and swept away the statue but the rock which had broken the statue grew and became a huge mountain filling all the earth.

Having told him what he had dreamed, Daniel then began to give Nebuchadnezzar the interpretation of the dream. You, Daniel told the king, are the head of gold to whom the God of heaven has given dominion and power and might and glory. After you, represented by the silver chest and arms, Daniel went on, will arise another kingdom which will be inferior to yours and then a third kingdom, represented by the bronze, and then a fourth represented by the iron legs (2:36-38).

Daniel especially spoke of the feet of iron mixed with clay. He said that this part of the story meant that this fourth kingdom would be a divided one and though it had the strength of iron, as it progressed through time, the kingdom would develop divisions, which would weaken it. Eventually, the stone cut without hands out of a mountain would eliminate these kingdoms and fill the whole earth.

Notice that the statue not only represented kingdoms but it also showed a time sequence as it progressed from head to foot. The kingdom represented by the head comes first, then another represented by the silver, then the bronze kingdom, and finally

27

the kingdom of iron legs and then that kingdom becomes divided. Daniel goes on to say that "In the time of those kings, the God of heaven will set up a kingdom that will never be destroyed nor will it be left to another people. It will crush all those kingdoms and bring them to an end, but it will itself endure forever" (2:44).

When Daniel had finished, King Nebuchadnezzar, the most powerful man of that day, who had great armies at his command and ruled with an iron hand, fell prostrate before Daniel and honored him. He said "Your God is the God of gods and the Lord of kings and a revealer of mysteries, for you were able to reveal this mystery" (2:47).

Remember that Daniel was only in his late teens, from a foreign country, and was probably just finishing the educational program Nebuchadnezzar had designed for him. The king, however, was so impressed with Daniel and his God, that he placed Daniel in a high position and lavished many gifts upon him. The king placed him over the entire province of Babylon and put him in charge of all of his wise men. And, at Daniel's request, he made his three friends, now called Shadrach, Meshach, and Abednego, as administrators over the province of Babylon.

This prophecy tells of coming world empires and of the kingdom of God. Later prophecies in Daniel will provide even more details of these coming empires, but we should note here that the Babylonian Empire was overthrown by the Medo-Persian Empire in 539 BC, a kingdom that was not as opulent as the head of gold. Then in 331 BC, the Greeks under Alexander conquered the Persians and thus came the belly and thighs of bronze. The fourth kingdom, the legs of iron, represents the powerful Roman Empire which began to conquer from the west toward the east, crushing everything in its path. In 63 BC, it took control of the land of Israel. Eventually, the Romans became weak within, iron mixed with clay, and eventually fell from both within and without. It was during the time of this empire that God Himself established a kingdom—the church, which began in 30 AD.

From Daniel's life, we can learn many important lessons. What led to this great outcome for such a young man? (1) He determined to obey God. We learned this in chapter 1 when he refused to eat food from the king's table. (2) He prayed and asked his friends to pray for God's help. When he knew the gravity of the situation, Daniel set his heart to pray and to ask others to join him. And (3), Daniel gave God the credit when he had success. When he went before Nebuchadnezzar to reveal the dream and to give the meaning God had given him, the first thing he told the king was that there is a God in heaven who can reveal mysteries. And Nebuchadnezzar understood because after the dream and interpretation were given, he said to Daniel: "Surely your God is the God of gods and the Lord of kings and a revealer of mysteries" (2:47). Here is a great pattern for us: Determine to obey God, pray for God's help to do the right thing, and then give God the credit when He helps us.

From the dream and its interpretation, there are important things for us to know. The four parts of the image represented four different kingdoms. We are told that the head of gold represents Nebuchadnezzar and the Babylonian Kingdom. Although the others are not named in this passage, from later prophecies in Daniel we shall study and from history, we can clearly identify the other three world empires. After the Babylonians came the Medes and Persians, then the Greeks, and then the Romans. Daniel 2:44 says that it would be during the days of this last empire, the Romans, that God Himself would establish a kingdom not like the other four. Although the first four were all physical kingdoms, the fifth kingdom would be a spiritual one. As Jesus told Pilate, "My kingdom is not of this world" (John 18:36). And, as God revealed to Daniel, this kingdom was established during the days of the Roman Empire.

So, during the time of the Roman Empire, a babe was born in Bethlehem who is Christ the Lord. When He was grown, this man preached that "the kingdom of heaven is at hand" (Matthew

4:12). And after His resurrection, he spent forty more days with his apostles teaching them about the kingdom of God (Acts 1:4). Then, on the Day of Pentecost in 30 AD (Acts 2), Peter preached for the first time the risen Christ. On that day, the kingdom was established, composed of all who were being saved (Acts 2:47; Colossians 1:13). Jesus had told His followers that the kingdom would be established during their lifetimes (Mark 9:1), and so it was. Thus, Daniel's prophecy came true: During the fourth of these empires, God Himself established a kingdom which would fill all the earth. And while that kingdom was growing, the earthly empire during which it came would decline and no earthly kingdom would ever again have the dominating power over the world, which the four kingdoms of Daniel's dream had.

In this way, the dream of Nebuchadnezzar, which Daniel revealed and interpreted for him, came to pass just as Daniel had said. But it came not through Daniel's own power; it came through the power of the God of heaven to whom Daniel gave the credit. In his day, Daniel could only reveal what would come in the future. From our day, however, we can look at what Daniel wrote and see that his prophecy came true just as he spoke about it—not by the power of Daniel, but through the power of God.

God intended the fulfillment of such prophecies 600 years after they were given and precisely as they were delivered to be evidence of His ability to foretell the future and His power to bring about His will. Today, this prophecy is evidence that God not only knows the future, but has the power to work within the will of human beings to see that His plan unfolds.

What personal applications can we make from this story of Daniel? There are three specific lessons from Nebuchadnezzar. First, when he realized that through the power of his God that Daniel had revealed and interpreted his dream, he fell prostrate before that God by falling before Daniel. Nebuchadnezzar was in awe of such power. So should we be in awe of such a God. The God we believe in is the Creator, Sustainer, and Ruler of the universe, yet He loves each one of us so much that He sent His Son to die for our sins. Such a thought should inspire us to want to return that love to Him. Sometimes we lose sight of how honored we are to be in the family of such a God. We go to worship but do not engage deeply in such songs as "Praise the Lord, Ye Heavens Adore Him" or "Our God Is an Awesome God, He Reigns from Heaven Above." When we pray, we may not recognize as fully as we should that we are entering the throne room of great majesty. As Hebrews 4:16 says, "Let us then approach the throne of grace with confidence, so that we may receive mercy and find grace to help us in our time of need."

Second, Nebuchadnezzar spoke aloud to honor Daniel's God. "Surely your God is the God of gods and the Lord of Kings" (2:47). On other occasions in Daniel, Nebuchadnezzar even publishes decrees that go throughout his kingdom to tell of his respect for God (3:29; 4:34-37). How often do we tell others of our belief in and respect for God? Do we hide our faith from our co-workers or share it with them? Do we share our belief in God and Christ with fellow students or fellow athletes or fellow club members or with neighbors down the street? Let's follow the example of Nebuchadnezzar and tell others of our great God and His Son, Jesus Christ.

Third, Nebuchadnezzar honored God by placing His servant, Daniel, in a high position. So, we should honor those who serve God. We should tell our ministers that we appreciate their work, not just by saying as we leave church, "Good sermon," but by sending a note or email or text message to tell why we appreciated the sermon. And ministers should keep a notepad on their desks to write a few thank-you notes every day to people in their congregation who have served God in a good way. Likewise, elders should send notes and bring deacons and others to their meetings to express their appreciation and pray for their work.

So, Nebuchadnezzar gave us a good example to follow in showing awe to God, in speaking to someone else about God, and in honoring God's servant.

Sermon Thoughts from Daniel 2

What God Can Do: Preparing the Way for the Lord

Develop a sermon from the five kingdoms which God predicts will come. The first four all played a part in His bringing about the arrival of His Son to establish the fifth kingdom.

1. The Babylonian Empire carried the Jews into captivity as God had predicted through His prophets. This captivity was punishment for their often going after idols. After the Babylonian Captivity, the Jewish people didn't worship idols again. This important development for the Jews prepared them to be the people through whom God could bring the promised Messiah.

2. The Medes and Persians conquered the Babylonians and early in their Empire, Cyrus allowed the Jews to return to their homeland. This return allowed them to rebuild their temple and re-establish their religion, another important preparatory step for the coming Messiah.

3. The Greeks conquered the Medes and Persians and spread their power further than any of the preceding Empires had done, and in so doing, they spread the Greek culture and language throughout the known world. Having a language people all over the world could use was an important tool for the writing and preserving the message of the coming Messiah. About 200 BC, all the Old Testament books were translated from Hebrew into Greek in what was called the Septuagint, and all the books of the New Testament were written originally in Greek so they could be read throughout the many nations of the Roman Empire.

4. Then came the Romans, building roads and making travel and trade easier throughout the world. They also brought a time of relative peace, which prevailed during the first-century AD. The common Greek language, the Roman roads,

and the time of peace made this century a good time for Christ to be born, live, die, and be raised so the message could be spread. And in reading the book of Acts, the story of the spread of the message, all of these factors are important. On Pentecost in Acts 2, people were gathered from "every nation under heaven" who heard Peter preach and who, then, took the message back home with them. Peter, Philip, Paul, Barnabas, Luke, and many others made use of travel, a common language, and general peace to spread the message.

Conclusion: Thus, Paul wrote that "when the times will have reached their fulfillment" God would bring together all things under Christ and that He had made this mystery known to those of his day (Ephesians 1:10). Daniel's prophecy of the four kingdoms, which would prepare the way for God's eternal kingdom shows how God enabled the times to reach their fulfillment for Christ to come. It is our job now to share with others how God worked His will to bring a Savior to make it possible for us to have forgiveness of our sins. If God would do all it took to bring Jesus at just the right time, we should be willing to do our part in spreading that message.

Follow Daniel's Plan for Obeying God's Will

Tell the story of Daniel 2, and then make the application that we should use the following process in our lives:

1. **Daniel determined to do God's will.** (We can do this by study and by sharing our plan within our families and with others we trust).

2. **Daniel prayed that God would help him.** (We can do this by our own prayers and by asking others to join us in prayer).

3. **Daniel gave God the credit for the good outcome.** (We can do this by thanking God for his answer to our prayers and by sharing with others the good things we have experienced through God).

Lessons from King Nebuchadnezzar

Use the thoughts above about the example of Nebuchadnezzar in showing awe to God, telling someone else about his respect for God, and doing something to honor God's servant.

CHART 1

Picture	Daniel's Interpretation	Further Interpretation
Head of Gold	Nebuchadnezzar / Babylonian empire	
Breast and Arms of Silver	Medes & Persians	
Belly and Thighs of Bronze	the Greeks	
Legs of Iron Feet/Iron and Clay	the Romans	
Stone Cut out Without Hands	eliminate the above kingdoms; fill the whole earth	
Smote the Image	feet of iron & clay	
Stone Became a Mountain	filled all the earth	

CHAPTER 3

Decision in the Plain of Dura

Daniel and his fellow Jews—Shadrach, Meshach, and Abednego—had been in their positions about fifteen years following Daniel's interpretation of the king's dream. As high-level government officials under Nebuchadnezzar, they would certainly have had the best living quarters, the finest clothing, and would have been held in the highest respect.

As Nebuchadnezzar enjoyed great success as ruler of the world's greatest empire of his day, stretching from Egypt and most of present-day Turkey back to Babylon and then to the east another five hundred miles, he became a great builder. He erected the magnificent hanging gardens, noted as one of the seven wonders of the ancient world, and the beautiful Ishtar Gates—an extraordinary entrance street and gate into the city. He also created palaces and government buildings, and then decided to build an image to worship in the Plain of Dura, outside of the city of Babylon.

As one would expect of Nebuchadnezzar, he spared no expense as he built a structure that was ninety feet high and nine feet wide. Think of something as tall as a nine-story building but only nine feet wide. The Bible does not give us all the details, but says that the monument was made of gold. It probably was built of glazed bricks, as were many things in Babylon, and then covered with gold. Think of how much gold it would take to cover an object whose surface was 3,240 square feet! The tall, narrow shape suggests that the image was likely an obelisk like so many monuments were in Egypt.

37

DECISION IN THE PLAIN OF DURA

When the image was completed, Nebuchadnezzar decided to hold a great dedication ceremony. He invited all of his subordinate government officials: satraps, prefects, governors, advisers, treasurers, judges, magistrates, and all the other provincial officials. Although we do not know the number present, those holding all these offices would have made a large crowd.

To make this occasion all he wanted it to be, Nebuchadnezzar decided he would have musicians with wind and stringed instruments to play and when the music started, everyone present was to "fall down and worship the image of gold"(3:5). The herald who gave these instructions to those present even said, "Whoever does not fall down and worship will immediately be thrown into a blazing furnace" (3:6). The command was given, the musicians played their instruments and "all the peoples, nations and peoples of every language fell down and worshiped the image of gold King Nebuchadnezzar had set up" (3:7).

There were, however, three men present who did not bow down: Shadrach, Meshach, and Abednego. These men were high-ranking government officials and had been for more than a decade. But they did not bow down to worship the image of gold. The monument represented a pagan god, and to them, worshiping the image would have been giving allegiance to an idol. They knew the Law of Moses said not to worship any kind of idol. With the great crowd assembled, all of whom were falling down before the image, these three stood out clearly. They had heard what punishment had been declared for not bowing before the great monument, but they were determined not violate the commandment of God.

Some among the king's wise men called astrologers noticed that these three stood up while everyone else was bowing down. They told King Nebuchadnezzar "...there are some Jews whom you have set over the affairs of the province of Babylon—Shadrach, Meshach and Abednego—who pay no attention to you, Your Majesty. They neither serve your gods nor worship the image of gold you have set up" (3:12).

Nebuchadnezzar was "furious with rage" (3:13). How dare these three officials not bow down according to his commandment! He quickly summoned them and asked "Is it true, Shadrach, Meshach, and Abednego, that you do not serve my gods or worship the image of gold I have set up?" (3:14). Then he told them he would give them another chance to bow down and if they did not, they would be thrown into the fiery furnace. "Then what god will be able to rescue you from my hand" (3:15)?

Worship the image or be burned alive in the furnace! What a choice Daniel's three friends faced! Then they responded to the king. "We do not need to defend ourselves before you in this matter. If we are thrown into the blazing furnace, the God we serve is able to deliver us from it, and he will deliver us from Your Majesty's hand. But even if he does not, we want you to know, Your majesty, that we will not serve your gods or worship the image of gold you have set up" (3:16-18).

They defied the king's order and stood firmly for what they believed. As they had done earlier regarding the king's food, they determined what their course of action would be and were ready to stand on that action regardless of the consequences.

Nebuchadnezzar was enraged that these three high-ranking officials in his government would defy his order to worship before his new, glorious monument of gold. He ordered that the furnace be heated seven times hotter than its usual temperature and then soldiers were to take them to the top of the furnace and throw them into the flames. When the furnace was ready, the soldiers took hold of the three and threw them through the top opening in the furnace. The heat there was so intense that the three soldiers who threw them in died from the extreme heat.

Nebuchadnezzar could see into the lower opening of the furnace, which was probably a kiln where bricks were glazed, thus having both a top and a lower opening and with variable temperature. And when he looked in he was amazed, "Weren't there three men that we tied up and threw into the fire? . . . Look! I see four men walking around in the fire, unbound and unharmed, and the fourth looks like a son of the gods" (3:24-25).

Then the king approached the opening of the furnace and shouted, "Shadrach, Meshach, and Abednego, servants of the Most High God, come out! Come here!" (3:26). And the three walked out of the fire unharmed!

What had just happened? The men who were thrown into a blazing fire that was likely hotter than 1,000 degrees Fahrenheit walked out unharmed. And a fourth person was seen in the furnace with them. Who was he? The Bible does not tell us, but the king called him "a son of the gods." Since the person would have been sent there from God as a protection, the person was either an angel or the pre-incarnate Son of God. There are several occasions when someone appears in the Old Testament who is described as "an angel of the Lord" but whose qualities are more than ordinary angels possess—thus having the qualities of deity. One of those appearances would be the third being that appears to Abraham in Genesis 18 and others could be the one who speaks to Moses at the burning bush in Exodus 3, and the one who wrestles with Jacob in Genesis 32. These stories all indicate that the Person present is worthy of worship which would not be proper for an angel. We are not told enough here to be sure but, in any case, God was sending a protecting agent to keep the three from being harmed.

As Shadrach, Meshach, and Abednego came out of the fire, those present crowded around them to see these men who had not been burned in the highly heated furnace. Even their clothes were not burned nor did they smell of fire. Nebuchadnezzar got the point. He said, "Praise be to the God of Shadrach, Meshach and Abednego, who has sent his angel and rescued his servants! They trusted in him and defied the king's command and were willing to give up their lives rather than serve or worship any god except their own God" (3:28). He went on to say that any in his kingdom who should say anything against their God should be cut in pieces and have his house turned into rubble "for no other god can save in this way" (3:29).

What a great demonstration of faith! These three men stood alone in front of a great crowd of the leading men of their day. They put their lives on the line rather than violate what God had told them. Live or die, they were going to stay faithful. And many others through the years have been willing to do this. Stephen, the first Christian martyr, died for his faith (Acts 7) and so did millions of other Christians during the early centuries of the church. Even in our day, we know of those who have died rather than renounce their faith, and we admire them for their stand. After all, what is this short life compared to what we shall have eternally? Much better to have this life cut short than to spend an eternity in hell for failing the test when so much is on the line.

For the second time in the book of Daniel, Nebuchadnezzar recognized the true God as supreme. He did it when Daniel told him what he had dreamed and interpreted it for him, and fifteen years later, he did it again when he recognized that the same God saved the lives of his administrators. Though we have no indication that he renounced his idols, he did recognize the one true God who can save people from the fiery furnace.

Obviously, we can learn great lessons from this stand for faith. When everyone at your company Christmas party is drinking intoxicants, what will you do? When you are tempted to engage in sexual sin, what will you do? When you are present when someone starts to tell a dirty story, what will you do? When your boss tells you to change the financial records to make the tax burden less, what will you do? When you are filling out your own tax records and could report less income than you really made, what will you do? When you are tempted to cheat on an exam, what will you do? When a link to a pornographic site comes up on your computer, what will you do? When someone angrily speaks ill of you, what will you do? When you have the opportunity to invite someone to church, what will you do?

If we consider that these men were willing to die to stand for their faith, they will serve as good examples for us when our faith is tested.

One of my favorite examples about standing for what you think is right is the story of a nurse who was assisting in an operation as the last event in her training. She had heard that the doctor with whom she was working was demanding, and she was trying to do everything right. The operation involved putting sponges in the patient's abdomen to absorb blood as the doctor was doing the surgery. She was to count the sponges as they were used so that she could be sure to count them as they came out. When the doctor was ready to close, she said to him, "There is one more sponge to find. I counted twelve going in, and I have only eleven here which have come out." The doctor replied, "Look, you are the nurse, and I am the doctor. I'll close when I am ready." She responded, "I know you are the doctor, but my job is to count the sponges, and I believe there is one more." "Don't you know that your future is in my hands," he responded. "If I say the word, you will not get your nursing license." "I know that," she said. "But this patient's health is at stake, and I believe we must find one more sponge." Then the doctor moved his foot and under it was the missing sponge. He was testing to check her resolve to do the right thing, and he gave her a high recommendation.

Take a moment to think of your greatest temptation to sin or to show a weakness of faith. Then ask yourself what you can learn from Shadrach, Meshach, and Abednego. Let their example stand firmly in your mind.

Sermon Ideas from Chapter 3

What God Can Do: Deliverance at Dura

1. Narrate the story with interesting detail—like storytelling.
2. Chose five or six situations in which to apply standing for

your faith in situations your members face and emphasize that just as God delivered the three from the furnace, God will deliver you if you stand for Him. Now this does not necessarily mean that you might not suffer loss or even death if you stand up for your faith. It does mean, however, that God will bless you in one way or another if you stand for right. If you have real stories to tell about the situations, use them. If you have to make up stories about how the situation might look and how you hope your members will handle it, that is satisfactory if you start the story with "It would be like this" or "So when you." This way the audience knows the story is realistic, but not actual. God knew stories were powerful tools. That is why He put so many stories in the Bible for us.

Always Stand for Your Faith

God put in the Bible many stories of people who did the right thing when they might have failed to stand for their faith. A good sermon could be made from telling several of these stories with good details using not only what is in the Bible but also using additional details from history, geography, and archaeology. Here are possible stories to tell that would match the story of Shadrach, Meshach, and Abednego: Abraham, Joseph, Joshua, Ruth, David and Goliath, Josiah, Esther, Nehemiah, Stephen, and many more. You could tell two or three of these stories and then tell two or three stories of people today who have stood for their faith—stories of people just like those in your audience.

What Lines Should You Draw?

The success of Shadrach, Meshach, and Abednego in meeting a temptation was fixed long before the event that put their faith to the test. Some fifteen years earlier they had met the situation they faced about the food with a commitment that they would not violate the teachings of the Law of Moses. So here is another situation—will they bow before an idol and worship? Having earlier made the commitment, they did not waver when the situation arose.

Here are principles to follow in drawing lines for yourself.

- Study Bible characters who drew the line like Joseph, the three Jews in Babylon, and Peter and John in Acts 4.

- Decide in advance where you will draw the line on such things as always telling the truth, on sexual matters, on responding to criticism, on not missing out on opportunities to share the good news.

- Pray that God will help you not to cross the line.

- Recognize that, in the long run, the benefits of holding the line are much greater than any possible benefits of crossing the line.

- When the moment of decision arrives, live your faith.

CHAPTER 4

The Mighty Has Fallen

King Nebuchadnezzar was a man of great achievements. He had led his armies in many conquests. He had built great palaces, the hanging gardens, and the great monument of gold that was ninety feet tall. He was the richest and most powerful man in the world. But along with great achievement comes the temptation to be proud and arrogant. And, as Daniel 4 shows, Nebuchadnezzar had fallen into that trap. This entire chapter, interestingly, is the only chapter in the Bible written by a pagan king. It is an official document which Nebuchadnezzar wrote to the peoples and nations over which he had control to tell them of his own experience in being brought low. So let's study this story of what God can do to humble the proud.

Nebuchadnezzar says that it is his pleasure to tell about the signs and wonders which the Most High God performed for him. He even says that this God has an eternal kingdom and his dominion endures from generation to generation. Thus, other kingdoms may rise and fall, but this God, whom he honors with this document, has a kingdom that never wanes.

Then the king tells that he was in his palace, contented and prosperous when he had a dream. He called his wise men to interpret the dream, but they could not tell him the meaning. Then Daniel came and Nebuchadnezzar asked him to interpret it. This time the king told Daniel what he saw. It was a great tree that was tall and its top touched the sky and it was visible to the ends of the earth. Its leaves were beautiful and its fruit abundant. It gave food for all and even animals under it were fed, and the birds sitting in its branches had plenty. Suddenly, a holy one came from heaven and said, "Cut down the tree and trim off its branches, strip off its leaves and scatter its fruit. Let the animals flee from under it and the birds from its branches. But let the stump and its roots, bound with iron and bronze remain in the ground, in the grass of the field" (4:14-15).

Then the voice of the one from heaven continued, "Let him be drenched with the dew of heaven, and let him live with the animals among the plants of the earth. Let his mind be changed from that of a man and let him be given the mind of an animal, till seven times pass by for him. . .so that the living may know that the Most High is sovereign over the kingdoms on earth and gives them to anyone he wishes and sets over them the lowliest of people" (4:15-17).

Nebuchadnezzar then says in his document that he asked Daniel to interpret the dream for him and reports that when Daniel understood the dream, he was greatly troubled. But he did reveal the meaning. Daniel told Nebuchadnezzar that the tree represented the king and how he had spread his kingdom to the distant parts of the earth and everything was flourishing. The words of the messenger about cutting down the tree, however, meant that the king would be cut down. But as the stump was left, so he would remain. For a time, he would live like a wild animal, however, until seven times passed by. This all meant, Daniel said, that the king would be driven away from people and live with animals until he acknowledged that the Most High was sovereign over the kingdoms and gives them to whom He will. Daniel then urged the king to "Renounce your sins by doing what is right, and your wickedness by being kind to the oppressed" (4:27). If he would show humility and unselfishness, Daniel said, then his prosperity could continue.

Daniel really wanted to help the king and gave him advice that would keep this dire tragedy from happening to him. As the king explains in his document, however, he did not follow

Daniel's advice. But, all went along as usual for twelve months, so it seemed there was nothing to worry about. But then one day, the king was walking on the roof of his palace in Babylon and viewing all he had built in the city. He swelled with pride as he thought about the great things he had done to make the city a monument to his wealth and glory. Then came a voice from heaven saying that his royal authority was taken from him and he would be driven away from people and live with the wild animals, even to the point of his eating grass like cattle. This edict from God will last until "seven times" should pass over him before he would acknowledge that the Most High is sovereign over the kingdoms of men.

All that had been spoken before happened to the king immediately and he began to live like an animal, eating grass and being drenched with the dew. Eventually, the document says, Nebuchadnezzar recognized that he must have a humble spirit, and he raised his eyes toward heaven. When he did, his sanity was restored, and he praised the Most High and honored Him. Then he was allowed to return to leading his kingdom, and he became even greater than before.

So that he could acknowledge his new recognition of God, he prepared the document quoted in Daniel 4 and sent it throughout his empire to tell everyone that he now recognized that he should praise and exalt and glorify the King of heaven "because everything he does is right and all his ways are just. And those who walk in pride he is able to humble" (4:37).

What an amazing statement from the ruler of the greatest empire of his time! He had worshiped pagan gods all his life and following an encounter with the Most High, he recognizes His superiority over the others. Notice the change in Nebuchadnezzar from Daniel 2. Then, he was quick to use his power to condemn to death his wise men because they could not do what for them was impossible—to tell the king what he dreamed. In Daniel 3, he was furious with Shadrach, Meshach, and Abednego because

47

they would not bow down, and he quickly condemned them to death. By Daniel 4, however, Nebuchadnezzar seems to have mellowed somewhat. Particularly after his time away, he does not lash out in anger but, rather, shows that he accepts God's "training program" for him and demonstrates a humble spirit.

Since most of the book of Daniel was written while the Jews were in captivity in Babylon, it is possible that they were questioning whether their God was as powerful as the gods of Babylon. When this decree was posted around the empire, it must have given them reassurance that their God was the truly great God.

So what do we learn from this event in the life of Nebuchadnezzar? First, we learn the danger of wealth and power. The king wallowed in his own greatness. He did things to build his own name. And we can have the same attitude. There is, of course, a satisfaction for having done something well and that is a good thing. But when this attitude grows to pride with a haughty and arrogant spirit and the desire to put others down so we may rise up, then we have developed a damaging pride. Success in athletics, in business, in preaching, in teaching, or anything else can cause a pride that leads us to think more highly of ourselves than we ought to think (Romans 12:3). Solomon said, "Pride goes before destruction, a haughty spirit before a fall" (Proverbs 16:18). Let's use Nebuchadnezzar's fall from pride to help us examine our own hearts so we can eliminate any spirit of pride.

A second lesson from Nebuchadnezzar's fall is the need for proper priorities. When Daniel interpreted the dream, he told the king how to avoid the terrible fate that awaited him: He should do what is right and be kind to the oppressed. In other words, king, quit thinking about all the nations you have conquered and the great things you have built, and set your mind on doing what is right and helping the poor. Change your priorities. This is another great lesson for us. We often put other things in our lives ahead of serving God. I remember, for example, a fine Christian young man in high school who did well in football and football became the focus of his life. He got a scholarship to a top NCAA team and played on the national scene, but he left his faith behind. Many have put their jobs above their spiritual life and fallen away from the faith. Others have let entertainment or sports or hobbies move them away from church attendance and Bible study.

A third lesson from Nebuchadnezzar's dream is that God gave him a call for change. Daniel told the king how to make the change without the drastic fall, but he ignored the advice. Only after suffering humiliation did he become what God wanted him to be. If we need to make improvement, that change will come one way or another. If we become what God wants us to be as we understand the need, then God will reward us for the change. But if we wait to honor Him and die in that condition, one day we will join everyone in bowing before Jesus and confessing His name (Philippians 2:10-11), but the change will have come too late to make an eternal difference.

A fourth lesson from Nebuchadnezzar's experience is the joy of humility. Once he finally got the point and humbled himself before God, the king was much greater than before and much happier. He admitted that "those who walk in pride he is able to humble" (4:37). In the long run, God will bless a humble life, and those who walk in humility will enjoy life more than the proud.

Sermon Thoughts on Daniel 4

What God Can Do: Bring Down the Proud and Exalt the Humble

Tell the story of King Nebuchadnezzar's being brought down.

The Dream, The Interpretation, The Fulfillment, The Confession.

Apply the principle of humility to life situations today by telling how to be humble in situations such as the following:

Humility as a boss

Humility as an employee

Humility as a parent

Humility as a child

Humility as a teacher

Humility as a student

Humility as a coach

Humility as an athlete

In the conclusion, mention how Jesus humbled Himself for our benefit as motivation for us to be humble (Philippians 2).

Pride or Humility?

James 4:6—God resists the proud, but gives grace to the humble.

- The proud walk in their own way while the humble obey the will of God.
- The proud want to enforce their will on others while the humble submit to those who have authority over them.
- The proud want to be served while the humble serve others.
- The proud want to be honored while the humble are willing to go unnoticed.
- God gives grace to the humble, but He withholds grace from the proud.

The Nature of God

God is Most High—He is above all, with all power, all knowledge.

God is Everywhere—Nebuchadnezzar sends his message to the whole world and God is omnipresent.

God is King—He has an eternal kingdom, and since He is king we must submit to Him. God was king of Israel (1 Samuel 8:7; 1 Chronicles 29:23), a physical kingdom. Christ is king of the new, spiritual kingdom open to all (Colossians 1:13, 18), God will be king of the eternal kingdom after Christ's return (1 Corinthians 15:24).

God is Involved—He knew about Nebuchadnezzar and expected certain qualities of him as a ruler and, likewise, he knows each one of us and expects certain qualities from us.

Lessons from Nebuchadnezzar's Dream (See above)
- The Danger of Wealth and Power
- The Need for Proper Priorities
- The Call for Change
- The Joy of Humility

The God Who Humbles Kings
- God humbled Pharaoh of Egypt with ten plagues.
- God humbled the King of Nineveh through the preaching of Jonah.
- God humbled Nebuchadnezzar through a time of mental illness.
- God humbled Belshazzar through defeat by the Persians.
- God humbled Herod Agrippa I through an attack of worms.

Conclusion: The God we serve is a mighty God, worthy of our praise and our submission.

and his face grew more pale (5:9). The queen, probably a surviving wife of Nebuchadnezzar and so really the "queen mother," heard about the problem and came to help Belshazzar. She remembered a man in the kingdom who had demonstrated "insight and intelligence and wisdom like that of the gods" (5:11). She was recalling Daniel who had been the chief of the wise men under Nebuchadnezzar and who had interpreted dreams for him. "Call for Daniel, and he will tell you what the writing means," she said (5:12).

So the elderly Daniel was brought before King Belshazzar who asked him if he was one of the exiles from Judah which, of course, he was. He repeated to Daniel the promise of the purple robes, the ornament, and the third place in the kingdom.

Daniel replied that he was not interested in the rewards, but he would read the writing for the king and tell what it meant. Next Daniel reminded Belshazzar of the time when the arrogance of his predecessor Nebuchadnezzar had brought him humbling circumstances. He had been deposed from his throne for a while, living like an animal until he "acknowledged that the Most High God is sovereign over all kingdoms on the earth and sets over them anyone he wishes" (5:21). Daniel implied, of course, that from such an experience and the decree that Nebuchadnezzar afterward had sent throughout his kingdom, that Belshazzar should have known not to be arrogant himself.

Then Daniel directly accused Belshazzar of a similar arrogance because he had set himself "up against the Lord of heaven. You had the goblets from his temple brought to you, and you and your nobles, your wives and your concubines drank wine from them. You praised the gods of silver and gold, of bronze, iron, wood and stone, which cannot see or hear or understand. But you did not honor the God who holds in his hand your life and all your ways. Therefore he sent the hand that wrote the inscription" (5:23-24).

Having clearly told the king what a mistake he had made in

GOD SENDS A MYSTERIOUS MESSAGE

desecrating the goblets intended for worship to God, Daniel was ready to proceed with reading the inscription and providing its meaning. He said the four words written on the wall were Mene, Mene, Tekel, Parsin. And then he explained what they meant. The word *mene* was the word for *numbered*, and Daniel applied this to Belshazzar and the Babylonian Empire. Its days were numbered and time for them had run out. Just to emphasize that point, the word appears twice.

The next word is *tekel,* which means *weighed*. So, said Daniel, "You have been weighed on the scales and found wanting" (5:27). This means Belshazzar's administration had not lived up to what God expected of it.

The final word is *parsin,* which means divided and from this Daniel said "Your kingdom is divided and given to the Medes and Persians" (5:28).

After Daniel interpreted the words for the king, Belshazzar kept his promise and proclaimed Daniel the third ruler in the kingdom. As Daniel knew, however, that position wouldn't last for long since "that very night Belshazzar, king of the Babylonians, was slain, and Darius the Mede took over the kingdom" (5:30-31).

Several ancient historians wrote about this important event: Herodotus in 450 BC, Xenephon in 360 BC, the writer of the Annalistic Tablet, and the incoming Persian King Cyrus, who left several records including the annalistic Tablet and the Cyrus Cylinder. These documents allow us to fill out the story. As the army of the Medes and Persians came to take the city of Babylon, they knew that the great wall with its moat would make it difficult to conquer the city as armies usually did. So they devised a clever scheme. Since the Euphrates River flowed under the wall, they found a way to divert the flow of the river so that the water level of the river under the wall would go down. And when the water was low enough for its soldiers to walk under the wall, they made their way inside without even a fight. There was no battle for the city at all, but they did kill the king that night, exactly as

Daniel says it happened.

And here is an additional interesting element. In Jeremiah 50 and 51, the prophet clearly describe the coming fall of Babylon. There he mentions several details of its demise. In 50:3, 9, and 41 and in 51:11, 28, he says the invader will come from the north and will be made up of a coalition of nations, even mentioning the Medes specifically. In 50:26 he speaks of Babylon's well-supplied storehouses and in 51:53, 58 he speaks of its towering fortifications. A particularly interesting verse is 51:36 in which Jeremiah speaks of her sea (the Euphrates River) being dried up, and 51:39, 57 speak of the event's happening during a feast. Jeremiah 51:8 uses the word *suddenly*. So from Jerusalem and nearly a hundred years before the event took place, Jeremiah predicted the fall of Babylon in clear terms.

Daniel 5, then, is truly an astounding record. It was correct about there being a king called Belshazzar well before the historical records of such a king had been found. It tells of one of the most significant events in world history, the transfer of power from the Babylonian Empire to that of the Medes and Persians and is exactly accurate in its statement that on the night of the feast, King Belshazzar was killed and the incoming power took control of the city without a fight.

And Daniel's example, again, provides great lessons for us. First, Daniel continues to serve God well into his eighties. We need to keep ourselves busy for the Lord no matter our age. We have all observed those in older years who are still active visiting shut-ins, having Bible classes in their homes, teaching in jails and prisons, making phone calls to those who need encouragement, writing books and articles, sending cards, preaching, teaching Bible classes, helping with classes for teens and children, driving people who need transportation, leading singing, and doing many other fine works. "Let us not grow weary in doing good, for at the proper time we will reap a harvest, if we don't give up" (Galatians 6:9).

Second, Daniel had clear priorities. He didn't serve the king because of promised royal robes, a chain around his neck, or even third place in the kingdom. He went to the feast to serve God as his first priority. What is our first priority? Is it serving God or is it having fun or making money or having the best looking home on the block?

Third, Daniel spoke clearly about sin even to the king. We need to speak clearly to those in sin to encourage them to follow the right path. We should speak the truth in love (Ephesians 4:15). Too often we either turn our heads the other way or join in with those who are sinning. We must take a strong stand against what is wrong as Daniel did, but always working with the best strategy to help people learn to do better.

Fourth, Daniel opens the message of God to those who need to hear it. God put the message on the wall of the palace dining room, but someone needed to explain it to those who needed it. Daniel provided this service. We often let opportunities to share the message with others slip by. There are Christians who have started Bible studies with a waitress who served them in a café, with their hairdresser, a bank teller, a fellow-athlete, a fellow-student, someone who works where they do, or with a neighbor next door. The opportunities are there if we will jump the hurdle of fear of rejection and make the effort.

Sermon Ideas from Daniel 5

What God Can Do: God Brings the Fall of Babylon

1. God Accurately Predicted the Fall of Babylon—Jeremiah 50-51.
2. God Brought Cyrus, the Person to Conquer Babylon—Isaiah 44:28; 45:1.
3. God Deposed Belshazzar Who Desecrated the Temple Goblets—Daniel 5:22-24.

4. God Brought Daniel Back as Power Changes in Babylon—Daniel 5:29; 6:1-3.

How God Deals with Sinners
   1. **God's punishment is not always immediate.** Sinners sometimes think they are able to defy God and His commands. Belshazzar, for a time, was enjoying his feast and drinking from the vessels of the temple. And many today sin and enjoy the pleasures of sin for a season.
   2. **God's punishment is always sure.** God did judge the sin of Belshazzar and brought him to defeat. Many stories in the Bible show God's punishment of the sinner—Adam and Eve, the people of Noah's day, the Israelites when they listened to the ten spies, Nadab and Abihu, King Saul, David and Bathsheba, King Uzziah, Ananias and Sapphira, just to name a few.
   3. **God's punishment is sometimes in this life.** Use some of the above examples.
   4. **God's punishment is final for the next life.** (Matthew 7:13-14; 24:36-25:46; Revelation 20:11-15).

Conclusion: Recognizing God's hatred for sin, we should walk in His paths, in the light, so He can take us to be with him. (1 John 1:6-8, Matthew 25:34; Revelation 20:11-15; 21:7-8).

Weighed and Found Wanting
   1. **Weighed in the balance.** Everyone is subject to the judgment of God for his life. Our lives are put on one side of the scale and God's own just law is on the other. Any departure from God's commands is crossing the line into sin and any sin takes the scales out of balance.
   2. **And found wanting.** Our words may condemn us (Matthew 12:36; 15:18-20). Our actions may condemn us (Galatians 5:18-20; Revelation 21:8). All have sinned (Romans 3:23).

GOD SENDS A MYSTERIOUS MESSAGE

   3. **But in Christ we have hope.** (Acts 2:38; 22:16; Galatians 3:26-27; Romans 5:2-5; 1 John 1:6-8).

Daniel is a Great Example (See above)

1. Daniel continues to serve God well into his eighties.
2. Daniel has clear priorities.
3. Daniel speaks clearly about sin even to the king.
4. Daniel opens the message of God to those who need to hear it.

CHAPTER 6

Faithfulness, Persecution, and Deliverance

The ruler under the Medo-Persian Empire, which had just conquered Babylon, is called Darius in Daniel 6. This may have been another name for Cyrus or may have been a subordinate. As he organized his new government, he decided an efficient method was to appoint 120 satraps or local officials to help. Rather than to have all of these report directly to him, he believed it would have served best to have three administrators over them. Apparently the king had heard of Daniel's effective work with Nebuchadnezzar and perhaps also of Daniel's proper interpretation of the handwriting on the wall, and so he selected Daniel, who was likely by this time in his mid-eighties, as one of these three major administrators.

As we would expect from what we have learned earlier about Daniel, he served extremely well. In fact, he so distinguished himself among the other officials that the king decided to appoint him over the other two administrators, thus making him the second in command over the entire empire. His "exceptional qualities" brought him this recognition. He never took bribes, and he carried out his work effectively and efficiently. He was fair in dealing with others. In short, he was highly successful in every aspect of his work.

The other two administrators, however, were unhappy that Daniel was to be elevated above them. Along with some of their satraps, they plotted against Daniel to try to prevent his appointment to this new role. They searched Daniel's conduct of governmental affairs to find some mistake or some corruption or some

FAITHFULNESS, PERSECUTION, AND DELIVERANCE

negligence, but they couldn't find anything of which to accuse him. Imagine! A man in such a high position, dealing with many different people, handling financial matters, and administering government policies, and yet they couldn't find even one situation in which he had not done his job to perfection. So, they decided, they couldn't keep the king from appointing Daniel to the new post by any charge about failure in his job. No wonder the king had decided to appoint Daniel to a higher position.

But those opposing Daniel did not give up. They recognized that Daniel's religion might give them an opportunity. After all, he worshiped a God who is different from the gods of other government workers. And there they found it. There was a practice of Daniel's which they believed would give them the opportunity they sought. They observed that three times a day Daniel went to his upstairs room where he opened his windows toward Jerusalem, got on his knees, and prayed, giving thanks to his God.

They finally had the opportunity they needed. They devised a scheme to make Daniel either change his practice of prayer or to violate a law. They knew Daniel well enough to think that he was not likely to change his practice of prayer, so that meant he would break the law. So they sought to get a law passed that no one should pray to anyone but the king for thirty days, not even their own god.

To carry out their scheme, the other administrators drew up a proposed law that said "anyone who prays to any god or human being during the next thirty days, except to you, Your Majesty, shall be thrown into the lion's den" (6:7). They then went to Darius and said that all of the king's administrators and other officials agreed that they wanted to honor the king with a decree that for thirty days no one could pray to anyone but him. This was not true, of course, because Daniel certainly had not agreed to it. Darius considered their proposal an honor to him, which he wanted to accept, and so he signed the document that made this decree the law of the land and, under their legal system, the law could not be rescinded.

Daniel's enemies thought they had what they needed to bring Daniel down as a law breaker. They watched his windows to see what he would do. Maybe Daniel would continue to pray, but do it where he couldn't be observed. He could pray in a closed room or lying in his bed, but behind closed doors. If he did so, his enemies couldn't prove anything against him and their plot would fail—after all, what could be wrong with praying privately?

Such, however, was not Daniel's approach. He did not want these men to believe they could affect his religious practice. He wanted them to know that he was totally committed to his God and that their subterfuge would not change his spiritual practice. He wanted to demonstrate to them that his relationship to his God was the most important thing in his life and so if that meant death, such was of small consequence in the long run.

Actually Daniel was following a practice Solomon had recommended more than three hundred years before. In dedicating the temple, he had said in prayer to God that the time might come when, because of their disobedience, God would take His people into a foreign land. If He did take them away, then the people should admit their sin and "pray toward the land you gave their ancestors, toward the city you have chosen." God would then hear that prayer and uphold their cause (1 Kings 8:48).

So Daniel walked into the trap set for him, knowingly and intentionally. He determined to put God first in his life and, if this meant punishment and even death, he was willing to face it.

With the evidence against Daniel in their hands, the other administrators rushed to the king and said, "Did you not publish a decree that during the next thirty days anyone who prays to any god or human being except to you, Your Majesty, would be thrown into the lions' den" (6:12). And the king replied that he had signed such a decree. Then they sprang the trap. "Daniel, who is one of the exiles from Judah, pays no attention to you,

FAITHFULNESS, PERSECUTION, AND DELIVERANCE

Your Majesty, or to the decree you put in writing. He still prays three times a day" (6:13).

When the king heard this, he was greatly distressed. He realized the plot laid against Daniel and spent all day looking for a way to keep from carrying out the penalty, but he found no escape for Daniel. He had signed the law, and it could not be changed. Daniel would have to be cast into the den of hungry lions.

"...and they brought Daniel and threw him into the lions' den. The king said to Daniel, 'May your God, whom you serve continually, rescue you!'" (6:16). Then they closed the den with a large stone and the king placed his seal on it so no one had the authority to release Daniel from what seemed certain death.

King Darius then returned to his palace and spent the night in anxiety. He fasted and allowed no entertainment. He could not sleep. He had deep appreciation for Daniel and felt terrible that he had been tricked into sending his favorite administrator into a deadly situation. At first light, the king made his way to the lions' den to find out what had happened overnight. He called to Daniel in an anguished voice, "Daniel, servant of the living God, has your God, whom you serve continually, been able to rescue you from the lions" (6:20)?

Then he heard Daniel's voice from inside the den, "'May the King, live forever! My God sent his angel, and he shut the mouths of the lions. They have not hurt me, because I was found innocent in his sight. Nor have I ever done any wrong before you, Your Majesty.' The king was overjoyed and gave orders to lift Daniel out of the den. And when Daniel was lifted from the den, no wound was found on him, because he had trusted in his God" (6:21-23).

There is so much we can learn from this event about Daniel's life!

1. **Daniel prayed.** He prayed regularly, he prayed often, he prayed fervently. Clearly Daniel's prayer life was a key ingredient in his fine character. In Daniel 2, he had prayed God would reveal Nebuchadnezzar's dream and in Daniel 9, we will read of

another prayer. Throughout the Bible, those who pray regularly and deeply are those who live the closest to God.

2. **Daniel projected.** His life in God was a clear statement to all who saw him. The king admired him because of his high character and service and even his enemies had to respect him for his unfailing integrity. We, likewise, need to project to others the high standards to which God calls us and the joy of living such a life. As Jesus said, we should let our "light shine before others, that they may see your good deeds and glorify your Father in heaven" (Matthew 5:16). Project the good life so that others will be drawn to it.

3. **Daniel prioritized.** There is no greater example in Scripture of one setting his priorities and living by them than Daniel. To him, doing what was right and keeping his contact with God through prayer were the most important things in his life, and not even threat of death could change that. His life shows the importance of our setting clear priorities in our life with God having first place. If we determine that we will make that commitment, then when events come along, as they will, we already will have made the decision—we will do what is right whatever the cost.

4. **Daniel persevered.** There was no ounce of quit in Daniel. He persevered through his entire life in doing what was right before God—he would not eat food that would defile him, he would always do the proper thing in his service to the king; he would not bow to pressure to stop praying. From his teenage years through his eighties, Daniel persevered. And so should we. Again, we must determine. We must set our hearts to follow Jesus. We must "walk in the light as he is in the light" and Jesus will keep on taking away sins (1 John 1:7). In fact, Peter says that those who have "escaped the corruption of the world by knowing our Lord and Savior Jesus Christ and are again entangled in it and are overcome, they are worse off at the end than they were at the beginning" (2 Peter 2:20).

FAITHFULNESS, PERSECUTION, AND DELIVERANCE

There's much to learn from this event in Daniel's life! His example is a great model for us to follow. In carrying out his work so honorably that nothing could be found against him, he shows us that we should give maximum effort to doing our jobs well. Even more than this, in carrying out his work, Daniel demonstrated to everyone around him his commitment to his God. The king knew the God whom Daniel served and called Him "the living God." Even his enemies recognized that Daniel put serving his God in first place. Daniel's example of praying three times a day surely encourages us to be people of prayer. And when he had to make a choice about his priorities—to be safe or to follow his commitment to God—he never wavered but put God in first place. Someday we may be faced with dying because of our Christian faith, and if so, we should be willing to die as so many of our fellow Christians have done since the first century. When, as is more likely, we are faced with decisions about priorities in our lives, we should be committed to putting God first. That means God comes first as we use our money, our time, and our talents. We can all think of people around us who have given up higher paying jobs to be ministers or missionaries, or who have gone to places of risk to serve God, or who have spent a night a week in visiting, or who have home Bible studies, or who have taught children's classes, or who have been faithful during trials of loss and illness.

Just as it has been during the 2,600 years since it happened, Daniel's story of faithfulness to overcome great obstacles still stirs and instructs us.

After receiving Daniel from the den of lions, King Darius determined to punish those who had plotted against his administrator in such a devious way. He commanded those who had "falsely accused Daniel" be thrown into the den of lions along with their wives and children. Although this may seem extreme in our time, it was the king's way of stating that devious plots against his officials were not to be tolerated.

Then the king sent a decree to all the peoples, nations, and languages throughout his empire which said that "in every part of my kingdom people must fear and reverence the God of Daniel. For he is the living God and he endures forever; his kingdom will not be destroyed, his dominion will never end. He rescues and he saves; he performs signs and wonders in the heavens and on the earth. He has rescued Daniel from the power of the lions" (6:26-27).

Such a strong statement of support for the true God of Israel from a leader of the great Persian Empire! He had worshiped idols all his life, but he finally saw the true God at work and he respected what Daniel's God had done.

Following this event, "Daniel prospered during the reign of Darius and the reign of Cyrus the Persian" (6:28). So Daniel was restored to his position and continued in it for a while. No details are given in the book of Daniel about when he died, but he lived at least through the third year of Cyrus because the revelation of Daniel 10 comes at that time.

Sermon Thoughts from Daniel 6

What God Can Do: God Shall Deliver the Righteous

1. **The Righteous Shall Suffer Persecution.** Daniel was as righteous as one can be, yet he had enemies. Satan attacked Jesus (Matthew 4), and he goes about as a roaring lion to attack Christians today (1 Peter 5:8). He will find ways to tempt us and draw us away often in ways that almost seem innocuous. Jesus said that we should be happy when people revile us and persecute us because that makes us like the prophets who went before us (Matthew 5:11-12). And Paul wrote that "everyone who wants to live a godly life in Christ Jesus will be persecuted" (2 Timothy 3:12). A Christian may be passed over in his job because he does not drink with his co-workers or a teenager may be ridiculed because

FAITHFULNESS, PERSECUTION, AND DELIVERANCE

she stands against her peers in their partying, or a college student may have a teacher who attacks him because he does not believe in evolution. In some cases, the attacks become even more violent, sometimes ending in death. From India recently there was the report of someone having been murdered by Hindu relatives after being baptized into Christ. There was also the story of a husband who poisoned his wife because she became a Christian. She survived. Her husband ultimately also converted to Christ.

2. **The Righteous Shall Be Delivered.** God delivered Daniel from the den of lions by sending an angel to protect him. Is God any less powerful today than He was then? In our day God has not chosen to work in the openly miraculously ways that He has in some times, but He works, nonetheless, through His providence on our behalf. We pray for wisdom to make a difficult decision and God can help. We pray for safe travel and God can help. We pray to be healed from illness and God can help. We pray for strength when we lose a loved one and God can help. He does not always give us what we request, but He is working on our behalf nonetheless. Sometimes God wants to use us as a demonstration of how Christians can deal with difficulties in a more positive way than non-Christians can. Have we not seen this and been encouraged by it so many times?

Use Daniel as Your Model (See above)
1. Daniel Prayed
2. Daniel Projected
3. Daniel Prioritized
4. Daniel Persevered

Daniel Was Constant
1. Constant Prayer
2. Constant Righteousness
3. Constant Trust
4. Constant Courage

CHAPTER 7

Four Beasts and a Son of Man

Daniel Chapter 7

As we begin chapter 7, we enter the second section of Daniel. The first six chapters have focused on events in his life; the second six chapters are focused on prophecies he received. He dated the prophecies by telling the year of the king in which he received the prophecy and these years reach back to the time of Belshazzar so the second half of the book overlaps the time of the first half.

As we look at these prophecies, we need to keep in mind that Daniel was in Babylon where God's people were in captivity for their disobedience. God wanted to send them an overall message of encouragement. We don't know just how Daniel shared these thoughts with the people. In fact, he was told to seal them up for the future. In any case, the prophecies did suggest that something better lay ahead for them.

The first of these four prophecies came to Daniel in a dream during the first year of Belshazzar, 553 BC, when Daniel had been in Babylon for fifty-three years and was about seventy years old. He was in bed at night when this dream came to him.

Daniel saw a great sea, like the Mediterranean, and a strong wind churning the water. One at a time, four large beasts came up out of the water, and Daniel saw each one of them in detail. The first beast looked like a lion which can fly with two wings like those of an eagle. Then suddenly its wings were torn off and it stood up on its two feet like a man and the heart of a man was given to it.

FOUR BEASTS AND A SON OF MAN

Then Daniel saw the second beast coming out of the sea. It looked like a bear, and it was raised up on one of its sides, chewing on three ribs. It was told "Get up and eat your fill of flesh!" (7:5).

The third beast Daniel saw coming up out of the sea looked like a leopard and on its back were four wings like those of a bird. This beast had four heads and was given authority to rule" (7:6).

Then Daniel saw the fourth beast as it came out of the sea—"terrifying and frightening and very powerful." It has large iron teeth crushing and devouring its victims and trampling underfoot whatever was left (7:7). This beast had ten horns. As Daniel thought on this picture, more action began: another horn, a little one, came up among the others and uprooteds three of them. "This horn had eyes like the eyes of a human being and a mouth that spoke boastfully" (7:8).

Then another scene happened in Daniel's dream. Before him were several thrones and on one of them the Ancient of Days took his seat. A court was set for judgment and the presiding judge was one whose clothing was white as snow [representing ultimate purity] and His hair was white as wool [representing ultimate wisdom]. His throne was flaming with fire and sat on wheels which are also ablaze. A river of fire flowed out before Him and He was attended by thousands upon thousands and even ten thousands upon ten thousands. Once the court was seated, the record books were opened and the court began its work.

This court stripped the first three beasts of their authority, but allowed them to live for a period of time. The fourth beast, which came up after the others, was killed and its body destroyed and thrown into the blazing fire.

Then, as the dream continued, Daniel saw one before him who

was like "a son of man, coming with the clouds of heaven. He approached the Ancient of Days and was led into His presence. He was given authority, glory and sovereign power; all peoples, nations and peoples of every language worshiped him. His dominion is an everlasting dominion that will not pass away and his kingdom is one that will never be destroyed" (7:13-14).

Having seen the vision, Daniel was troubled so he approached one of those standing there in the vision and asked him what all of this meant. And he told Daniel the meaning.

First the angel gave Daniel a quick summary of the prophecy: The four great beasts represented four kingdoms that would rise up, but the saints of the Most High would receive a kingdom and would possess it forever. But Daniel asked for more details about the fourth beast "with its iron teeth and bronze claws—the beast that crushed and devoured its victims and trampled underfoot whatever was left" (7:19). He also wanted to know more about the ten horns and the little horn that came up after the ten horns and which spoke boastfully.

Then Daniel began to see still more action in the vision. The little horn "was waging war against the holy people and defeating them, until the Ancient of Days came and pronounced judgment in favor of the holy people of the Most High, and the time came when they possessed the kingdom" (7:21-22).

The angel then gave Daniel additional explanation. The fourth kingdom would devour the whole earth, crushing all others before it. Thus it would be larger than any of the other three. The angel said the ten horns represented ten kings from this kingdom and the eleventh, the little horn, would subdue three of the other kings. This one would speak against the Most High and oppress His saints and subdue them for a time, times, and half a time.

Then the court acted to take away the power of this last king and would destroy it forever. The power of the kingdoms was then handed over to the saints and the people of the Most High would participate in an everlasting kingdom.

Daniel was so overwhelmed by this dream and its interpretation that he was deeply troubled and his face turned pale. Although Daniel was given the vision and the outline of its meaning, he was not told exactly what the rising powers represented. He was told enough, however, that by studying the history of the world and some other related passages of Scripture, we can understand the future events God was revealing through this vision to Daniel.

First, let's recall the dream of King Nebuchadnezzar, which Daniel previously had interpreted in chapter 2 because there are strong parallels. In that dream, the king saw an image with four sections—a head of gold, chest and arms of silver, belly and thighs of brass, and legs of iron with feet of iron and clay and with ten toes. Daniel was told that the head of gold represented Nebuchadnezzar and the Babylonian kingdom. From history we saw that the Persians, Greeks, and Romans followed. Then came a stone representing a kingdom from God, which would destroy the image and fill the whole earth.

In Daniel 7, similarly, came four beasts representing four kingdoms to be followed by the kingdom from God. There were five elements in each, and they matched one another closely. This parallel helps us to interpret Daniel's dream in chapter 7. The lion with wings of an eagle would, thus, represent the Babylonians, who frequently used lions in decorating their walls of glazed bricks. Nebuchadnezzar had quickly spread his power and so the lion moved quickly. Then there came a time when, according to Daniel 4, that Nebuchadnezzar was stripped of his power and humbled, represented by the wings being torn off. Following that, the lion has the heart of a man and Nebuchadnezzar was restored after his period of humility.

The bear with one side higher than the other here represented the Medes and Persians with the Persian side higher because they were the more powerful element. This power conquered the Babylonians in 539 BC and then moved further west. The bear is pictured as eating ribs in its mouth because it devoured as it went forward, overcoming other nations both east and west of Babylon. Thus, it had its fill of flesh.

Next Daniel saw a leopard with four wings, representing the rapid spread of the Grecian Empire. Alexander conquered so quickly that by 33, he had no more worlds to conquer. Then Alexander died, probably of some kind of disease, on June 11, 323 BC. Alexander's son, however, did not inherit the kingship. His empire, rather, was divided among four of his generals, matching the four heads on the leopard.

The fourth beast did not look like any particular single animal. It was huge and powerful and completely dominated everything it faced with its ten horns, iron teeth, and brass claws. Such a description fits the Roman Empire quite well. This kingdom was much larger than any of the others, dominating not only the Mediterranean World but even conquering Europe, including the British Isles. Its power was so strong that from shortly before the birth of Christ until two centuries after, the world experienced relative peace called the Peace of Rome or *Pax Romana*.

The ten horns are said to represent ten kings and we can best understand them by learning about the eleventh horn, the little one. This horn will speak against the Most High and oppress His saints and the saints would be handed over to him for a time, times, and half a time (7:25). Then the court where God sits will take away his power.

So what do the ten kings represent and who is the little horn? Since we may be sure that the fourth kingdom is the Roman Empire, we can be sure that these eleven kings are connected with Rome. Since the book of Revelation also deals with the Roman Empire, representing it as a beast with seven heads and on the seven heads ten horns, we can get some help from that book in understanding this "little horn" mentioned by Daniel. The best point of connection is to note that Daniel's little horn persecutes the saints and Revelation says this Roman beast was, likewise, "given power to wage war against God's holy people and to conquer them" (Revelation 13:7).

Revelation 17 gives more details about the seven heads of the beast. According to a common view, these represent the first seven emperors of Rome beginning with Augustus, 27 BC, and going through Titus, 81 AD. John, who records the vision, reports that five of these seven kings have fallen, one is in power at the time he writes, and the other has not yet come (17:10). Since one of them is in power at the time Revelation is being written, we know that these heads/kings were leading the Roman Empire during the first century. Then John writes about an eighth head, which is still to come and who belongs in some way to the first seven. Recall that the beast with these horns represents Rome, which persecutes the church, and the fifth head, Nero started the Roman persecution. If Nero is the fifth, that would make the eighth to be Domitian (82-96 AD) who was the second emperor to persecute Christians. Since the eighth is said to belong to the first seven, he would be like Nero coming back to life with his persecution.

Now another interesting point. In Daniel's vision, the persecuting little horn is the eleventh horn. In Revelation, Domitian is the eighth emperor but this is not counting three Roman rulers who served for less than a year each. Had they been included, Domitian would be the eleventh just as in Daniel.

There is another element of similarity between the beast of Daniel chapter 7 and Revelation's beast which stands for the Romans. Daniel says the saints will be handed over to the "little horn" for a "time, times, and half a time" (7:25). In Revelation 11, 12, and 13, a similar period of time is mentioned for Rome's oppression of the saints, that is Christians.* Revelation uses a "time, times, and half a time" for this period of persecution in 12:14, and refers to the same period as 1260 days (11:3; 12:6) or forty-two months (11:2; 13:5). Since 1260 days and forty-two months would both equal three and a half years, we note that "time, times, and half a time" would also equal three and a half years, if a time equals one year, times equals two years,

76

and half a time equaling half a year. Since we are dealing with this expression in a figurative context, we would not expect the persecution actually to be just for three and a half years but, rather, for some period of time represented by that symbol.

But what actually happens during this period? In all of these references in Revelation, the people of God are under persecution. Since Daniel's time, times, and half a time also refer to a time of persecution of the saints under an oppressing king, these are seen to be parallel occasions. This Roman persecution of Christians actually lasted about two hundred years, and some estimate that as many as six million Christians might have been killed during that time.

Daniel uses "horns" in his descriptions while John uses the figure of "heads." Both mention saints being persecuted for the same figurative period of a time. Now the beast in Revelation does, in addition to its heads, also have ten horns. These, however, are said to signify "ten kings who have not yet received a kingdom [at the time John writes], but who for one hour will receive authority as kings along with the beast. They have one purpose and will give their power and authority to the beast" (17:12-13). So, from this description we learn that the ten horns on the Revelation beast represent lesser kings yet to come in the Roman Empire after the time John writes Revelation and who will submit to those running the Empire. Thus, as is sometimes the case, the same element in one prophecy does not necessarily match exactly the same thing in a different prophecy, particularly when the descriptive details are different.

So, back to Daniel 7. Four world Empires are in view: Babylon, which existed when Daniel was writing; the Medes and Persians, which would take down Babylon in 539 BC; the Grecian Empire under Alexander, which would conquer the Persian Empire by 333 BC and then split into four subsequent kingdoms; and the Roman Empire, which would arise to be the largest of them all and was in power when Jesus came to earth. Under the time of the Romans, God says, will come a "little horn" who will oppress the saints of God and the saints will be handed over to him for a time, times, and half a time. Eventually, however, when God has achieved His purpose through the persecution, the heavenly tribunal will rule against this persecuting power, bringing it to defeat. Following this, God's kingdom will become an everlasting kingdom. Back in Daniel 2, the stone cut out without hands represented that during the days of the Roman Empire "God of heaven will set up a kingdom that will never be destroyed" (2:44) and here in chapter 7, one like a son of man approaches the Ancient of Days who gives him authority, glory and sovereign power in a kingdom that will never be destroyed (7:13-14). So from both chapters 2 and 7, we learn that God's new kingdom will start during the time of the Roman Empire, will be everlasting, and will fill the whole earth (2:44).

In Nebuchadnezzar's dream, then, there were four earthly kingdoms and a divine one, and in Daniel's dream, there were four earthly kingdoms and a divine one.

Kingdom	Daniel 2	Daniel 7
Babylon	Head of Gold	Lion with Wings
Medes/Persians	Chest and Arms of Silver	Bear Eating Ribs
Greeks	Belly and Thighs of Bronze	Leopard with Wings
Romans	Legs of Iron/Feet of Iron and Clay	Beast with Iron Teeth
Kingdom of God	Stone Cut Out—Destroys Statue	Son of Man Comes

This prophecy of Daniel 7 was written in 553 BC and told of events that would take place over the next six to seven hundred years. Ultimately, everything happened exactly as Daniel said it would. Another three major world empires arose to follow the Babylonians and during the fourth one, God endowed "the son of man" with a kingdom that would never end. In Acts 2:36, Peter, speaking on the first Pentecost after Jesus' resurrection, declared that God had made Jesus both Lord and Christ—He has become king of the new kingdom, the church, which was established on that day.

As noted below in the sermon thoughts, there are many practical lessons we can learn from this chapter in Daniel. This prophecy about coming world powers and its fulfillment as nations rise and fall during the coming six hundred years tells us so much about God. He works among the affairs of men. He uses the decisions they make as a part of His overall plan to achieve what He desires. He even uses the persecution of His people to achieve good ends.

When we think about such power and wisdom, we are struck by two things: the greatness of the God we serve and the thrill of recognizing that this great God cares about us personally. The kingdom He said He would establish during the reign of the fourth of these great empires, Rome, is composed of those who have accepted the sacrifice His Son made when He came to earth to rescue people from the clutch of Satan. What a joy to be part of this kingdom, which God foresaw so many years before it actually began! I should be so moved by this thought that I will do all I can to bring others to the knowledge of this kingdom.

Sermon Thoughts from Daniel 7

What God Can Do: What is God Like?
1. **God is eternal.** He is called the Ancient of Days (7:9).
2. **God is pure.** His clothing is white as snow (7:9).
3. **God is all-knowing (omniscient).** His hair is white like wool suggesting that He has the wisdom of years (7:9).
4. **God is present everywhere (omnipresent).** His throne has wheels suggesting that He moves throughout the universe (7:9).

5. **God is all-powerful (omnipotent).** A river of fire flows out from His throne (7:10).
6. **God is majestic.** Thousands and even tens of thousands honor Him (7:10).

Such a God loves me and wants to be with me, and I can only respond with thanks and obedience.

The Bible Is the Word of God.
1. **The Bible's references to history are accurate.** When Belshazzar was unknown to history, Daniel accurately spoke of his being a king who was second in the kingdom (he offered Daniel third place.) The Bible's description of the fall of Babylon to the Medes and Persians was accurate when compared with ancient historians. The Bible's description of Nebuchadnezzar as a great builder of the city of Babylon is accurate (4:30).
2. **The Bible predicts the future accurately.** In Daniel 7, we have an example of how a book written long before the events took place accurately told what would happen. (See the Appendix for more on this point.) And there will be more examples of this accuracy in later chapters of Daniel.

God Judges Now and Then

The Ancient of Days sits on a throne to judge from the record books that are opened. God is the great judge and considers our deeds as He judges.

1. God judges as we move through this life to bring consequences of our actions, even in this life (7:26). See Proverbs 5:22 and Galatians 6:7.
2. God judges when we come to the final judgment day (Revelation 20:11-15).
   a. **His judgment is universal**—everyone is present.
   b. **His judgment is fair**—based on our deeds.

c. **His judgment is final**—those judged go immediately to where He sends them.
  d. **His judgment is gracious**—those written in the book of life are forgiven of their sins and go into eternal life.

The Kingdom of God
  1. God will establish a new kingdom. God had a physical kingdom in the days of Israel (1 Samuel 8:7; 1 Chronicles 29:23). It was a kingdom over territory with armies, taxes, and laws. But Daniel 2:44 and 7:13-14 suggest that God will establish a new and different kingdom at some future date. This would be a spiritual kingdom.
  2. God will establish this kingdom in the days of the Roman Empire—the fourth of the great empires. (Daniel 2:44; 7:13-14).
  3. God will give this kingdom to the "son of man" (7:13-14). This was a term Jesus used frequently for Himself. (Luke 9:58; Mark 8:31).
  4. God will make Christ both Lord and Christ (Acts 2:36).
  5. God will add the saved to this kingdom (Acts 2:47; Colossians 1:13). Thus, the new kingdom is the church, established during the days of the Roman Empire.
  6. God will someday receive the kingdom back from Christ and will reign through times eternal (1 Corinthians 15:22-26; 2 Timothy 4:18).

God and Persecution
  1. **God sometimes allows persecution of His people.** He allowed the Jews to be carried into captivity. In Daniel 7:25 the prophet is told of a coming persecutor of God's people who shall "oppress his saints." This little horn, as shown above, is a reference to Emperor Domitian of the Roman Empire who reigned from 82 to 96 AD. He and Roman

Emperors who followed, persecuted Christians for about 200 years until Constantine brought the time of persecution to an end in 313 AD. During this time, a host of Christians were killed, some saying as many as six million.

2. **God used this persecution to spread the church.** Although the persecution was terrible in many ways, it brought so many to see the church in a positive light. The book *The Rise of Christianity* by Rodney Stark traces how the good lives of Christians, even while being persecuted and their courage in the face of death, brought many to want to know more about this religion. He estimates that by 350 AD there were thirty-four million Christians. Great persecution brought great growth. While Satan used persecution in seeking to destroy the church, God used it to help spread the church.

3. **God can bring the persecution to an end as He chooses.** In Daniel 7:26 the court sits and takes away the power of the persecutor and destroys him. And so the Roman Empire was destroyed after God had used it for his purposes. God's power is complete even though He may allow evil people to prevail for a time.

4. **God will greatly reward His saints who are persecuted.** Following the time of persecution, the kingdom of Christ prevails and is a kingdom that shall last forever (7:14). In Revelation 20:4-6 those who have been martyred for their faithfulness during the Roman persecution are said to have the reward of living and reigning with Christ for a thousand years.

CHART 3

Picture	Daniel's Interpretation	Further Interpretation
Lion coming out of the sea		
Eagles wings.		
Wings plucked.		
Stands as a man.		
Bear coming out of the sea.		
Raised up on one side.		
Three ribs		
Devour much.		
Leopard coming from the sea.		
Four wings		
Four heads		
Dominion given		
Fourth beast out of the sea		
Terrible, strong		
Great iron teeth		
10 horns		
Little horn comes.		
Eyes of a man		
Speaks great things.		
Made war with saints.		
Eventually fails. Saints possess kingdom.		
Throne placed for Ancient of Days.		
Throne on wheels.		
One like Son of Man comes to take kingdom.		

CHAPTER 8

The Ram and the Goat and the Future

Daniel records another vision God gave him, this time in the third year of Belshazzar, 550 BC, three years after the one recorded in chapter 7. At this time, Daniel was no longer one of the primary administrators, but had some lesser duties (8:27). In his vision, Daniel was transported to Susa, a secondary capital city about 230 miles east of Babylon, and the city where Esther would live about seventy-five years later. Standing beside the Ulai Canal of that city, he looked up and saw standing beside the canal a ram with two horns. The first horn to arise was surpassed by a second horn that came up later and was larger. The ram charged toward the west and north and south and overpowered everything before him. "It did as it pleased and became great" (8:4).

As Daniel was thinking about the ram, suddenly he saw a goat coming from the west, moving so swiftly that he was not even touching the ground. He had a prominent horn between his eyes, like a unicorn. The goat came toward the ram and charged it with great rage, attacking furiously and shattering the ram's two horns. Having taken away his power to defend himself, the goat then knocked the ram to the ground and began trampling him to destruction.

The goat then became great, but at the height of his power, his large horn was broken off and was replaced with four prominent horns. Then out of one of these horns came another horn, which started small but then grew in power to the south and to the east and toward the Beautiful Land. It grew until it reached the host of the heavens and threw down some of the starry host and

THE RAM AND THE GOAT AND THE FUTURE

trampled them. This horn, which grew out of one of the four original horns, took away the daily sacrifice and the place of the sanctuary was brought low. "Because of rebellion, the host of the LORD's people and the daily sacrifice were given over to it," and this horn prospered in everything it did, and truth was thrown to the ground. (8:12).

Then one angel spoke to another angel and asked how long all of this would take, to which the angel replied it would take 2,300 mornings and evenings, then the sanctuary would be reconsecrated.

In this vision, as in chapter 7, Daniel saw animals representing various entities, but he had no idea what these things meant. Then an angel, appearing in human form, called to Gabriel, one of the chief angels, asking him to tell Daniel the meaning of the vision. Six hundred years later, this same angel, Gabriel, announced the birth of John the Baptist to Zachariah and the birth of Jesus to Mary. In Daniel's vision, as Gabriel comes close to him, Daniel was terrified and fell prostrate before him. Gabriel, however, raised him up and said he would tell him the meaning of the vision as it relates to the future.

"The two-horned ram that you saw represents the kings of Media and Persia" (8:20). Thus, the horn that came up first but was not as large would represent the Medes while the horn that came up second but became larger would be the Persians. Since this kingdom was from the east, it conquered to the north, south, and west—going as far as present-day Turkey and even into Egypt. In Nebuchadnezzar's dream in Daniel 2, this kingdom was represented as the chest and arms of silver and in chapter 7 it was the bear chewing on three ribs. The Persians, under Cyrus, conquered Babylon in 539 BC and would continue as the major force in the world for about two hundred years. They would be important to the Jews because, after conquering the Babylonians, they allowed the Jews to return to rebuild Jerusalem and the temple and, eventually, the walls of the city.

Next in Daniel's vision he had seen a goat with one prominent horn. This goat would come with amazing speed to defeat the ram. Gabriel tells Daniel that the goat represents Greece and the single horn stands for its first king. And, of course, Greece under Alexander, the prominent horn, came with great speed to defeat the army of the Medo-Persian Empire. The major defeat occurred at the Granicus River in 334 BC and from there, Alexander conquered on to Babylon where he died on June 10, 323 BC, while lying in the palace of Nebuchadnezzar. Thus, the prominent horn was broken.

Gabriel then said that this one leader would be replaced by four as the one kingdom became four, none of which would be as powerful as the original one had been. And there could be no clearer statement of what happened. Alexander's kingdom did not pass to his posterity but to four of his generals: Cassander, Lysimachus, Ptolemy, and Seleucius. With Ptolemy in Egypt and Seleucius in Syria, their wars with each other often involved the land of the Jews which lay between them. Daniel 11 predicts even more details of these conflicts.

Daniel 8 then turns to give particular attention to one of the descendants of Seleucius whom Gabriel described as a wicked, stern-faced king: "He will cause astounding devastation and will succeed in whatever he does. He will destroy the mighty, the holy people" (8:24). He will take his stand against the Prince of princes but then he will be destroyed, but not by human hands.

As described earlier in the chapter, this same person, who grew from one of the four major horns as "a rather small horn," would come against the Beautiful Land, which in the mind of Daniel's readers would be the land of the Jews (8:9). He stopped the regular sacrifices and threw down the place where the sacrifices were offered. In doing these things, he served as God's agent to chastise His people because of their "transgressions."

Although Gabriel does not specifically identify this king, the clues are sufficient to do so. He is Antiochus IV called Epiphanes

THE RAM AND THE GOAT AND THE FUTURE

who ruled from 175 to 164 BC during the period between the Testaments. Though Daniel gives more details about this king in chapter 11, he appears here as one who would bring devastation to the Jews. Because they had not been faithful to God, He brought consequences to them, as happened so many times in the Old Testament. Antiochus sought to spread the Greek civilization with its gods, language, and customs. He worked with some among the Jews who were agreeable to such a change and took over the Jewish temple where he banished the sacrifices to God and erected an altar to Zeus.

Antiochus had a powerful army. In 166 BC, for example, he held a parade in which 46,000 foot soldiers marched, among them a Macedonian phalanx of 20,000 men and 500 mercenaries equipped with Roman arms, followed by 8,500 horsemen and 306 armored elephants.

About that same time, however, Judas Maccabeus began a rebellion against Antiochus. Because he gave attention to matters in other parts of his large empire, the revolt was successful and led to the cleansing of the temple and the restoration of the sacrifices. Following this, for a period of about a hundred years, the Jews were free from outside oppression until the Romans conquered them in 63 BC.

When Daniel asked how long the sacrifices would be prohibited, he was told for a total of 2300 days and nights. Though there is not total agreement over the exact length of time this number represents, it likely suggests a period of about three to four years during which Antiochus stopped the sacrifices.

After Gabriel had given Daniel the interpretation about the Persians and the Greeks and the "little horn" Antiochus IV, he told Daniel to seal the vision, because it concerned the distant future (8:27). Daniel wrote that after this vision he was exhausted and lay ill for several days but then got up and went about the king's business.

Below is a chart that compares the three prophecies of Daniel we have studied so far. Note the comparisons of the various symbols used to represent the same empires.

Kingdoms	Daniel 2	Daniel 7	Daniel 8
Babylon	Head of Gold	Lion with 2 wings	
Medo-Persia	Chest and arms of silver	Bear, higher on one side, eating 3 ribs	Ram with 2 horns, last is greater
Greece	Belly and thighs of bronze	Leopard moving with 6 wings and not touching the ground	He-goat with one horn, broken, then 4 horns in its place. Then little horn goes against God's people
Roman	Legs of iron and feet of iron and clay	Beast with iron teeth/bronze claws	
God's Kingdom	Stone cut out of a mountain	Son of Man comes to Ancient of Days	

Again, we see what a remarkable person Daniel was. God entrusted him with some of the most specific predictions of the future that He ever gave to anyone, even sending to him the high-ranking angel, Gabriel, to explain the meaning in specific terms. Daniel was so moved by this encounter that he lay ill for several days, but then got up and went about his work as usual.

As we have established by information in the Appendix, the book of Daniel clearly was written before the time of his death about 534 BC, yet from this vision God gave him, he writes with complete accuracy what will happen through 166 BC. Only through the power of God would such foreknowledge be possible.

Daniel's example for us shines through each chapter of the book. God used him as a conduit to spread His message. We, likewise, who have also received God's message through the Bible, which came as the Holy Spirit inspired men to write, should also

THE RAM AND THE GOAT AND THE FUTURE

be a conduit for the spread of God's message. We can do this when we share the good news about Jesus and His church to others. Daniel was also a good, consistent employee. Under two of the greatest monarchs of all time, he was their prime minister. When not in that role, he still served well. In our work, whatever our job may be, we should serve in such a way that those around us will notice our fidelity, honesty, and kindness so that they will, through our good lives, be drawn to know what causes us to serve so well.

Sermon Thoughts from Daniel 8

What God Can Do: Who God Is.

1. **God demonstrates His omniscience.** In accurately revealing the future to Daniel, God proves that He exists and that He knows everything. If He can know the future, He knows all.

2. **God demonstrates His judgment of the disobedient.** When His people disobeyed Him, God used foreign leaders to punish them. "Because of rebellion" God brought the foreign ruler on the Jews (8:12). Moses made a statement about what would happen if the Israelites failed to keep God's commandments, particularly about idols. In the book of Judges, over and over God brought outside forces on the Israelites to make them recognize their sin and need to repent. See Deuteronomy 31:14-22; Judges 2:10-23; Jeremiah 32:29, and other similar passages. Thus, God shows His power over all nations and, in so doing, demonstrates His omnipotence.

3. **God demonstrates His desire for truth.** Daniel 8:12 speaks of truth being "thrown down to the ground." God's people departed from His truth in pursuing a culture that involved idols and a different lifestyle than God commanded for the Jews. In departing from truth, they incurred God's wrath.

So today, God has revealed His truth for the Christian age—how people are to be saved, how they are to worship, how they are to live, and how they are to work together as a church. He is not pleased today when anyone throws truth to the ground.

Use Daniel as Your Example

1. **Daniel was a conduit for God's message.** Just as God gave Daniel a message to share with others, God has given us a message to share with others. His message dealt with informing people about future events while our message deals with sharing the gospel of Jesus. Our message is certainly as important as his and maybe even more important because one could go to heaven without knowing of Daniel's message, but cannot go to heaven without knowing about Jesus. Let's work hard to spread the message God has given us to share by being good examples to our neighbors and co-workers, thus preparing the way to invite them to events at church or to Bible studies. Let's participate in the evangelistic work at church by greeting visitors at church and following up with them.

2. **Daniel was a good employee.** For many years, he was the chief aide to Nebuchadnezzar, the most powerful man in the world. Then along came other kings and he was demoted, but he "went about the king's business" (8:27). Whatever his role was, he did it well. We should likewise do well in our work. Several passages in the New Testament speak about how well slaves should perform their work. Though we are not slaves today, the principle of doing your work well still applies. (See Ephesians 6:5-9; Colossians 3:22-25; 1 Timothy 6:1; and 1 Peter 2:18).

3. **Daniel was moved by receiving a message from God.** After Daniel received the prophecy, he was exhausted and lay ill for several days (8:27). Daniel was moved by receiving

the message from God. It is easy for us to read the Bible or to hear a sermon and, because we have done that so many times before, to let important thoughts slip by us almost unnoticed. We should pay careful attention when we can learn God's message so we can apply it to our lives. Are you moved by a message from Scripture or by a song with a biblical message? Like Daniel, we should be deeply moved when we receive a message from the Creator of the universe.

CHART 5

The Ram and the Goat From a Study of Daniel 8

Picture	**Daniel's Interpretation**	**Further Interpretation**

Ram
  Two horns.
  Higher came up last
  Pushing west.
Goat
  Came from west
  Didn't touch ground
  Notable horn
  Smote ram.
  Trampled
  before river.
  Magnified himself.
  Great horn broken.
  4 horns came up.
 	
From one horn comes a "little horn"—glorious land.
Cast down stars
Took away the continual burnt offering.
2300 days.
Then cleansed		

CHAPTER 9

Seventy Sevens and the Coming Messiah

By daniel 9, the time has moved forward fourteen years to 539 BC. The Medes and Persians had just conquered Babylon, and Daniel wrotes this message in the early days of Darius the Mede, the son of Ahasuerus. This Ahasuerus was not, of course, the same as the one Esther married, which would be nearly a century later. The handwriting on the wall and the instant defeat of Belshazzar was still fresh in Daniel's mind because it happened only a few months before. We can't tell for sure whether Daniel's rescue from the lions had just happened or was shortly to come.

Daniel has been reading his Bible, particularly the prophecy of Jeremiah. There in chapter 25, verses 11-12, the prophet predicted that Babylon would take the Jews into captivity but that after seventy years, they would be allowed to come back. We don't know just how Daniel got the words of Jeremiah, but we do know that Jeremiah had sent a letter to the exiles in Babylon after the second group was taken captive in 597 BC. Daniel may also have been aware of Isaiah's words in 44:28 where he prophesied of Cyrus as the one who would allow the Jews to return from Babylon. Now, with the Medes and Persians in charge, Cyrus has come on the scene.

As he read the message about the Jews being allowed to return after seventy years, Daniel was aware that this time was approaching. He and other captives had been taken in 605 and at this point in Scriptures it was about 539 or 538 BC. Daniel was struck by Jeremiah's words. He knew that God would keep His promise because He always does but, if the Jews had not repented of the sins that caused God to send them to Babylon, then He would be under no obligation to bring them back.

As he always had, Daniel turned to prayer, speaking to God in an impassioned way, and from his words, we learn much about Daniel, about prayer, and about God. As Daniel asked God to bring His people back, he went about it in an interesting way.

First, Daniel honored God by praising Him as "the great and awesome God, who keeps his covenant and love with those who love him and keep his commandments" (9:4). Later he said, "The Lord our God is merciful and forgiving" (9:9).

Second, Daniel confessed the sins of his people, the sins that caused them to be carried into captivity. "We have sinned and done wrong. We have been wicked and have rebelled; we have turned away from your commands and laws. We have not listened to your servants the prophets, who spoke in your name to our kings, our princes and our ancestors, and to all the people of the land" (9:5-6). Later in the prayer, Daniel continued his confession saying the people had been unfaithful, rebellious, disobedient, transgressors, and sinful. It was an open and deep confession of the sinful things the Jews had done.

Third, Daniel praised God as righteous. Daniel expressed to God that He was right to punish the sins the leaders and the people had committed. He even referred to the words in the Law of Moses (Deuteronomy 28:64) where God had said that if the people went after idols, He would send them out of the land and into captivity. And, as Daniel said in his prayer, the consequences of their sins had brought disaster to Jerusalem, and God was righteous in doing what He did.

Fourth, Daniel made his request. Having praised God, having confessed sins, and having praised God as righteous, Daniel next made his appeal. "Lord, in keeping with all your righteous acts, turn away your anger and your wrath from Jerusalem" (9:16). And "do not delay" (9:19). Daniel was specific in making his heartfelt request to God that the people could return.

Daniel: What God Can Do

Fifth, Daniel reasoned with God. It was not enough for Daniel to make a request from God; he also told God why He should respond to the request. You "made for yourself a name" when you brought your people out of Egypt so "in keeping with your righteous acts" bring back your people so that Jerusalem and your people will no longer be "an object of scorn" (9:16). Daniel said God should answer his request for the people to return and rebuild Jerusalem because that would be good for God's name. Daniel gave good reasons to God for why He should answer his request. It would be good for God and His reputation to answer the request.

Sixth, Daniel made a final appeal to God. "We do not make requests of you because we are righteous, but because of your great mercy. Lord, listen! Lord, forgive! Lord, hear and act! For your sake, my God, do not delay, because your city and your people bear your Name" (9:18-19). So Daniel said that it would be good for God if He would answer Daniel's prayer.

What a great example of prayer for all of us! Praise, confess, honor, request, reason, and appeal. We rarely reason with God about our requests, but if we can say that our request is something that will help God's church, exalt God, or bless His people, then we can share with God why it is a good thing for Him to answer our requests.

Having made his appeal to God about fulfilling the promise in Jeremiah, Daniel quickly received a response. Gabriel came to him again. He told him that "As soon as you began to pray, a word went out" (9:23). And the answer given to Daniel reassured him that the Jews would be allowed to return to their land, but much more than that was included in the response. Much of what the angel told him is meaningful from our vantage point, even though Daniel would not have understood the details of what the prophecy meant.

Gabriel told Daniel that "seventy 'sevens' are decreed for your people and your holy city" (9:24). Although some seek to make this time period to be exactly 490 years—seventy times seven—it is probably better to see use of "seventy sevens" in a more symbolic sense as a projection of general times and events rather than exact years.[1]

The angel then listed six aims to be accomplished by the end of this extended period of time (9:24). Since the angel told Daniel that after sixty-nine of the sevens "the anointed one will come" (9:25), we can be sure that this prophecy points toward the Messiah's arrival. Specifically, the angel gave Daniel six objectives, somewhat overlapping, to be achieved by the end of the seventy weeks and all of these related to the coming of the Messiah and His accomplishing what He would come to do. (1) "To finish transgression." The Messiah comes to restrain people from transgressing God's law. Thus, when one becomes a follower of the Messiah, he will not only be less likely to sin, but will also have a means of forgiveness for transgression. (2) "To put an end to sin." The Messiah will be the last actual sin offering and so will make it possible for people to end sin in their lives since they will be in a state of forgiveness. (3) "To atone for wickedness." The Messiah will be the ultimate sacrifice for sins. "With his stripes we are healed" (Isaiah 53:5; Hebrews 9:15). By taking undeserved punishment, He will free us from the punishment we deserve. (4) "To bring in everlasting righteousness." The Messiah will bring with Him the possibility of eternal salvation and He will bring people who obey Him to an everlasting righteousness. Jesus demonstrated His righteousness by living a sinless life. When He died, the righteous for the unrighteous, He made possible our reconciliation to God. In 2 Corinthians 5:21, Paul writes that "in him we might become the righteousness of God." (5) "To seal

---

[1] Some use the decree of Artaxerxes I in 457 BC as the decree to rebuild and, starting at that point and moving forward 490 years, moves to 27 AD, the time when Jesus began His ministry. A problem with this approach, however, is that if the last seven is considered as seven years, then Jerusalem would need to be destroyed seven years later or in 34 AD, but the destruction was not until 70 AD. Thus it would appear that the best plan for looking at the seventy sevens is to treat them as a symbolic time, which provides a generally shorter time of seven sevens for Jerusalem to be rebuilt, a long period of sixty-two sevens to wait for the coming Messiah, and then a shorter time of one seven for the Messiah to come, be cut off, and for Jerusalem to be destroyed again.

up vision and prophecy." In the Messiah, a host of prophecies would be fulfilled and, in addition, with His coming and the revelations given through Him and His apostles, there would be no need for additional revelation for God's message will have been fully revealed. Thus, when Christ's work and the work of the apostles He chose as His ambassadors was finished, there would no longer be any need for more revelation through prophets. We now have in written form the revelations given through the New Testament prophets and since no more revelation is needed, there is no longer a need for prophets to reveal it. (6) "To anoint the most holy." There can be little doubt who "the most holy was" in this section about the coming Messiah. This expression could only refer to deity and that deity would come in the Messiah who would be the Son of God. The anointing He would receive on earth was not just someone's pouring oil on Him, but the anointing God gave Him from His completion of the process of the death on the cross and His resurrection from the dead.

Having considered the six objectives to be achieved by the end of the seventy periods of seven, we now look to the event Daniel was told would mark the starting point of this series of events. The seventy sevens began when the decree went forth to rebuild the city, and the seventy periods ended when the city would be destroyed again. Thus the good news to Daniel was that Jews would get to return to their city and rebuild it. The bad news was that after seventy sevens, the city would be destroyed again. We can be certain that the prophecy was about a rebuilding and then a destruction that lay far beyond Daniel's time because Jesus referred to this prophecy in Matthew 24:15 when He spoke of a destruction of Jerusalem soon to come. He said, "So when you see standing in the holy place 'the abomination that causes desolation,' spoken of through the prophet Daniel." In the passage, He goes on to give more details about the fall of Jerusalem and, in Luke's account of this same sermon, Jesus urges people to flee Jerusalem when they see an army coming to surround it (21:20).

The angel said that the seventy periods of seven, sometimes called "weeks," would be divided into three segments. The first one  would begin when the decree went forth to rebuild the city and this was followed by the first seven sevens out of the seventy. That Cyrus issued such a decree allowing the Jews to go home is certain, and it was given sometime between 538 and 536 BC because in 1879 searchers found a cylinder in the ruins of Babylon on which Cyrus himself left a record of this decree. (That cylinder is in the British Museum.)

The ending event of this first period of seven sevens was not specified in the prophecy, but since Gabriel mentioned that the city would be rebuilt with "streets and a trench" (9:25), we would assume that this period ended when the rebuilding of the city of Jerusalem and the temple were complete. This time would have been about 430 BC after the temple was rebuilt and Nehemiah had led in the rebuilding of the walls and Ezra had led in re-establishing the law.

Next in the prophecy came the second of the three periods, and it constituted sixty-two periods of seven. This middle period began with the completion of the rebuilding of Jerusalem, about 430 BC and continued until the coming of the Anointed One. So, the Anointed One came at the end of sixty-nine periods of seven or, to put it another way, He came to begin the last seven of the seventy sevens. In this last period, several important things happened. The Anointed One was active during this time. Sometime in this seven He was cut off and had nothing. Also in the midst of this seven, the Anointed One confirmed a covenant with many and in the middle of the seven He put an end to sacrifice and offering. And when Jesus came, He, indeed, was cut off and had nothing. And through His death, He also put an end to the Jewish system of sacrifices and offerings because He became the ultimate sacrifice toward which the Jewish system of sacrifice had been pointing. They offered lambs, but He was the ultimate lamb. The blood of bulls and goats cannot take away sin, but Jesus' sacrifice does (Hebrews 10:4; 2 Corinthians 5:16-21).

Gabriel's forecast about the Messiah, then, offered not only insights about when He would come but provided a description of the important work He would do. He would achieve all six of the objectives mentioned, He would be cut off through His crucifixion, and His sacrifice on the cross would put an end to the need for any additional sacrifices for sin.

The angel also told about what would happen to Jerusalem in this last seven: "The people of the ruler who will come will destroy the city and the sanctuary. The end will come like a flood: War will continue until the end and desolations have been decreed.... And at the temple he will set up an abomination that causes desolation, until the end that is decreed is poured out on him" (9:26-27). Let us note several specific details given here of the destruction of Jerusalem and the temple. First, a ruler would come to do it. Titus was the son of the then-current Roman Emperor, Vespasian, and he became the next emperor. In fact, his father died while he was at Jerusalem, and he returned to Rome to claim his position as emperor. Second, the end came like a flood. Titus laid siege to the city on April 14, 70 AD but there was strong resistance from more than 20,000 defenders within the city. So while Titus was able to capture the northern section of the city, the rest of the city he held under siege for several months to starve out the people. By this strategy, he would lose fewer soldiers because the people would become too weakened to resist. Since Titus closed around the city during the time of Passover, some half-a-million people were inside the city. They quickly ate all the available food supply and were starving. Finally, he made his move when he knew the resisters would be weak. He stormed the city, conquering it section-by-section. By September 8, 70 AD, he had the city under his control. During the siege and conflict, tens of thousands either starved to death or were killed by Roman soldiers—a lot like the coming of a flood, just as predicted. After conquering the city and the temple, he took out some of the temple furniture to take it to Rome as a prize of victory, and then he totally destroyed the temple itself, taking down the stones and throwing them into the valleys below. Much of the city was burned to the ground. So, the historical record of the destruction of Jerusalem clearly matches the prophecy Gabriel gave Daniel.

We should also take note of what Jesus said about this prophecy of Daniel. According to Matthew 23:37-24:35, Jesus was in the temple courts, when He told the Jewish leaders that because they were rejecting Him, as their fathers had done with many earlier prophets, their house would be left desolate. The apostles then brought His attention to the temple building and courts; Jesus said, "...not one stone here will be left on another; everyone will be thrown down" (Matthew 24:2). Jesus was predicting the complete destruction of the temple and the city and said it would happen to that generation, those then listening to him (24:34). As He discussed this with the Jews, He also said, "So when you see standing in the holy place the abomination that causes desolation, spoken of through the prophet Daniel...then let those who are in Judea flee to the mountains" (24:15-16). At this same point in the message, according to Luke 21:20, Jesus even said, "When you see Jerusalem being surrounded by armies, you will know that its desolation is near."

So, Jesus knew about Daniel's prophecy, quoted it, and applied it to the coming destruction of Jerusalem, which He also predicted.

Here now is a summary of our study of Daniel 9.

1. Seven Sevens	2. Sixty-two Sevens	3. One Seven
Rebuilding Jerusalem	Intervening Years	Messiah comes Jerusalem destroyed

Gabriel through Daniel made accurate predictions about Jerusalem: It would be rebuilt, there would be a long intervening period, followed by the coming of the Anointed One who, although He would be cut off would bring an end to Jewish sacrifices. Following that would come a foreign leader who would totally destroy the temple and the city. And it happened just as Daniel had predicted.

Daniel 9, then, has a meaningful prayer from which we learn much about how we should pray, as noted above. It also contains marvelous predictions about the rebuilding of Jerusalem and its eventual destruction again, soon after the Messiah would come. Jesus' quotation of this prophecy lends to its significance and helps us to interpret it.

Sermon Thoughts on Daniel 9

What God Can Do: God Punishes and Restores
1. God Punishes the Disobedient
    A. He sent the disobedient Jews into Babylonian Captivity.
    B. He destroyed Jerusalem because of the disobedient Jews.

2. God Restores the Repentant
    A. He restored the Jews after the Babylonian Captivity.
    B. He received Jews who would accept Jesus (Acts 2).

What Daniel Teaches Us About Praying (See above)

Daniel's Life a Model to Follow
1. **Daniel's Early Determination.** In chapter 1, when he was only a teenager, Daniel had determined to do what was right. Our young people need such a determination to follow God's will.

2. **Daniel's Perseverance.** Throughout his life, even into his eighties, Daniel met every situation with the same

determination and dedication. He never wavered about doing what God would have him to do. All of us should set our hearts to persevere throughout our lifetimes.

3. **Daniel's Faith.** When faced with the difficult situation about the threat of being cast into the lion's den if he continued to pray, Daniel believed that if he did the right thing, God would deliver him. Although God does not always keep us from suffering and even death when we are faithful, we can always know that God will bless those who have faith in Him. When we face the hardships of life, as all of us will, we should demonstrate the faith of Daniel to believe that God will find a way to bless us.

4. **Daniel's Service.** Daniel always served his king well, so well that he was the prime minister to two of the world's most powerful monarchs. Christ calls us to a life of service to Him, to His church, and to those around us. We each need to find specific ways to use our talents for the Lord.

5. **Daniel's Light.** Even in the midst of those who worshiped idols, Daniel always let his light shine, even to the point that kings sent a message throughout their kingdoms that Daniel's God was to be honored and respected. Whatever our walk in life, we have opportunities to live before those around us so they will know of our faith and respect our manner of life.

6. **Daniel's Unselfishness.** When Daniel prayed the prayer in the early part of chapter 9, he spoke on behalf of his nation in a way that expressed their guilt. Though he did not partake in the sins which he mentions, he unselfishly speaks on behalf of others. We need to show unselfishness within our families, our friends, our recreation, and even our communities.

7. **Daniel's Prayers.** Over and over in the book of Daniel,

Daniel shows himself to be a man of prayer. He prayed three times each day and, no doubt, for some length of time. His other good qualities likely are due to his sense of closeness with God. We should likewise develop a prayer life that not only enables us to make our petitions to God, but allows us to express our love, honor, and appreciation for God and to include Him in our daily walk.

Choices in the Book of Daniel

By the time we get to chapter 9, we have seen many events, which have involved choices and the example of what decisions were made provide good direction for us. This set of ideas could be preached as one sermon or a series of sermons.

1. **To eat or not to eat.** Under all the circumstances Daniel faced, he had to decide whether to eat the king's food or determine to eat only what would not defile him. After all, he was in the midst of a new land where all but he and his friends followed the idols of the land. Should he really have absolutely refused to eat the food provided and, thus, risk his life over what he ate? Daniel determined that he would not eat defiling food whatever the cost and was true to his commitment (Daniel 1).

2. **To bow or not to bow.** In Daniel 3, we read the story of Daniel's companions, Shadrach, Meshach, and Abednego who were at a huge event where hundreds did as they were told and bowed before the great new image. Should they really stand out in the crowd by standing up when all around them were bowing? They were told that they would be thrown into a furnace to face what would appear to be sure death if they did not. Yet, they were determined to do what God would have them to do, believing that God would find a way to save them. Whether or not He did, they would follow His command not to worship idols.

3. **To pray or not to pray.** In Daniel 6, a law was passed that says no one could ask anything of any god or man except of King Darius for thirty days. Should Daniel risk his life by continuing his practice of praying to God three times a day with the window open toward Jerusalem? Maybe he could find a secret place to pray and no one would know. Daniel determined to pray just as he always had even if it meant being thrown to lions. And God delivered him from the mouth of the lions.

4. **To plead or not to plead.** In Daniel 9 we learn that Daniel had been reading the words of Jeremiah where God has promised that the Babylonian Captivity would last seventy years. Should he remind God of that promise and ask Him to fulfill it? Would it have been presumptive to remind God of what He had said and beg Him to live up to it? Should Daniel have pleaded the case of his people or just leave it in the hands of God? Daniel determined to find an interesting way to carry the case before God. He praised Him, confessed to Him, reminded Him, pleaded with Him, and reasoned with Him.

From these four occasions, we should discover what is the right thing to do, determine to do the right thing, and when the occasion arises, act in harmony with what we have determined.

The Anointed One

1. **The Anointed One Will Come.** Though the specific date for the Anointed One to come was not given, that He will come is clearly proclaimed.

2. **The Anointed One Will Be Cut Off.** He will not end His life as a ruler, but rather will be rejected (Isaiah 53:3-4). His own people will turn against Him and call for Him to be crucified. They cut Him off.

3. **The Anointed One Will Be a Ruler.** Some translations say "a prince." It is interesting that when Jesus was on earth, He was not a ruler. He held no office, had no money, and was even despised and rejected. Yet on Pentecost, Peter declared Him to be "this Jesus whom you crucified, both Lord and Messiah" (Acts 2:38). Colossians 1:15-20 declares Him to be creator, over all creation, and head of His body, the church.

4. **The Anointed One Will Put an End to Sacrifices.** Since the time of Cain and Abel, people had been making animal sacrifices to God—Abel, Noah, Abraham, David, Solomon, Elijah, and many others even down to the time of Jesus. With the coming of the Anointed One, however, the last valid sacrifice would be offered to God. All the other sacrifices pointed to the coming of the sacrifice of Jesus on the cross (Hebrews 9:12-14).

5. **The Anointed One Will Confirm a Covenant.** God has often worked through covenants with His people—Noah, Abraham, Moses and his people, and David. The coming Anointed One would confirm a new covenant which is the gospel message Jesus taught His apostles to teach (Hebrews 9:15).

CHART 7

The Seventy Sevens
From the Rebuilding of Jerusalem
Until Its Destruction Again

```
1    2                                      3  4  5
|____|_____|__|__|
```

7 sevens   62 sevens   1 seven

1. The decree to build the temple and the city. Probably in 538 BC. Some Jews return from Babylonian Captivity to re-build.

2. The conclusion of the building of the city. Probably about 408 BC when Nehemiah and Ezra complete their work of rebuilding the walls and reestablishing the law.

3. The Anointed One comes after the completion of the 62 sevens period to start the last period of sevens. This would be the beginning of Jesus' ministry in 26 AD.

4. The Anointed One is cut off in the middle of the week. Jesus was crucified in 30 AD.

5. The destruction of Jerusalem when a prince comes. Jesus refers to this passage when predicting the destruction of Jerusalem will come during the lifetime of those listening to Him (Matthew 24:15, 34). Titus comes on the wing of abomination to fulfil this part of the prophecy.

The six objectives to be achieved before the end of the seventy sevens are:
1. To finish transgression
2. To make an end of sins
3. To make reconciliation for iniquity
4. To bring in everlasting righteousness
5. To seal up vision and prophecy
6. To anoint the most holy

CHAPTER 10

Daniel and Angels

It had been two years since Daniel's last recorded vision, so chapter ten begins in the year 536 BC. Thousands of Jews had returned to their homeland, but many had chosen to stay in Babylon. One day, Daniel was given a revelation about the future of his people involved in a great war. Daniel was so stricken by the message that for three weeks he fasted by eating only simple foods. He prayed for more information about the vision so he could understand it.

For three weeks Daniel sought to know more about the vision and, finally, an angel came to him. He was standing on the banks of the Tigris River and when he looked up, there stood "a man dressed in linen, with a belt of fine gold from Uphaz around his waist. His body was like topaz, his face like lightening, his eyes like flaming torches, his arms and legs like the gleam of burnished bronze, and his voice like the sound of a multitude" (Daniel 10:5-6).

Daniel saw an angel whose appearance was striking. Although the description was similar to that of Jesus when He appears to John in Revelation 1, we know the one Daniel saw was not the pre-incarnate Jesus because an opposing angel had held him up for three weeks as he was trying to get to Daniel. According to Hebrews 1, Jesus is higher than the angels, so no angel could keep him from getting through to Daniel.

As Daniel looked at this vision of this beautiful angel, he lost his strength, turned pale, and felt helpless. Then the angel touched him and lifted him up and told him that he was "highly

109

DANIEL AND ANGELS

esteemed" (10:11). The angel went on to say that, because Daniel had prayed for understanding and had humbled himself, the angel had been sent to him in response. The angel said, however, that he had been delayed by the prince of the Persian kingdom who held him up for twenty-one days until Michael, one of the chief princes of the good angels, came to help him get through. Now that he had arrived, the angel told Daniel that he would explain to him "what will happen to your people in the future, for the vision concerns a time yet to come" (10:14). God was going to reveal more of His will about the future so people would know His Word and would know how to respond to it.

Daniel bowed with his face toward the ground and the angel touched his lips. Then Daniel could speak and said to the one standing before him, "I am overcome with anguish because of the vision, my lord, and I feel very weak. How can I, your servant, talk with you, my lord? My strength is gone and I can hardly breathe" (10:16). Again the angel touched Daniel to give him strength and said, "Do not be afraid, you who are highly esteemed" and then he said, "Peace! Be strong now; be strong" (10:19).

With that encouragement, Daniel felt stronger and asked the angel to speak more to him. The angel then said he would soon "return to fight against the prince of Persia, and when I go, the prince of Greece will come; but first I will tell you what is written in the Book of Truth" (10:20-21). Then the angel says that no one supported him against these two princes except Michael, your prince. And in the first year of Darius the Mede, I took my stand to support and protect him" (10:21-11:1). Then the angel proceeded to tell Daniel details about the future.

Chapter 10 is a prelude to the prophecies in chapters 11 and 12 and, though chapter 10 contains little in predictions about the future, it does give us interesting information about Daniel and about the work of angels.

From this section, we learn that God regards Daniel as "highly esteemed" (10:11). Although such a view was highly encouraging

110

to Daniel, it can also encourage us. God keeps up with His people and knows them. He knows us, He cares about us, and is aware of whether we are trying to do right. Though none of us will likely match Daniel for obedience, we can believe that God knows when we do right and is pleased. Jesus said, for example, that "Whoever acknowledges me before others, I will also acknwledge before my Father in heaven" (Matthew 10:32). Understanding that God knows us individually should motivate us to honor Him. The most powerful force in the universe knows us!

Another characteristic of Daniel from this chapter is that he had humbled himself before God and, because of that, God heard his prayer (10:12). "God opposes the proud, but shows favor to the humble" (1 Peter 5:5). Daniel showed humility in chapter 1 in the way he treated his superiors by asking with respect that he have a different diet so he would not defile himself. Daniel also showed humility in the presence of Nebuchadnezzar and Belshazzar as he dealt with them. Daniel was the number two leader in two of the world's greatest empires, the Babylonians and the Persians. A person holding such roles would certainly be tempted to think highly of himself. Yet, even when some of his subordinates attempted to find something against him, they couldn't—he had never mistreated anyone or used his authority in an inappropriate way. And, after they got him thrown into the den of lions, we never read that he sought retaliation against them although the king brought them retribution. Whatever our role, we should act with humility whether that means on the job, with our children, with our parents, in church matters, and even when we drive our cars.

Daniel was a man of deep spiritual dedication. When he wanted to know the meaning of a revelation given him, he spent three weeks praying and fasting in an effort to learn more. And, of course, we know he prayed on many other occasions as well. Early in his life, Daniel showed deep dedication to God, and this close connection continued throughout his life. An intimate

DANIEL AND ANGELS

personal relationship with God keeps us focused in our faith and in our obedience.

Another topic we learn about from Daniel 10 is angels. Although many of our questions about angels will not be answered until we live with them after this life, the book of Daniel gives more insights about angels than almost any other book of the Bible. The angel who visited Daniel in chapter 10 told him he had been trying to get to Daniel for three weeks but was hindered by the prince of Persia. Since an angel could not be hindered by a human prince, the reference here must be to some other angelic force and, since a higher ranking angel finally got him through, there certainly is a struggle between bad angels or demons and good ones. We also learn that there are ranks among angels thus giving some more power than others. Clearly there is a spirit realm in which angels exist and, in that realm, there is a struggle going on about people on the earth.

Three other passages give us a glimpse into this spirit world. In the book of Job, for example, God and Satan fought over Job. Satan said that God had so protected Job that it was easy for him to do right. So, God allowed Satan to harm Job, but within limits so he could not kill him. From this we learn that God and Satan are at war over people on the earth, that God has the upper hand, and that even though bad things can sometimes happen to good people, God will enable the faithful to come out well in the end.

Another passage that helps us learn about angels is Ephesians 6:10-18, which describes the armor Christians can wear. Interestingly, wearing most of the pieces traces back to knowledge of the Word—belt of truth, breastplate of righteousness, feet shod with the gospel, the shield of faith, the helmet of salvation, and the sword of the Spirit, which is the Word of God. Firm grounding in the Word allows us to take our stand against the devil's schemes because our struggle is against the rulers, authorities and powers of this dark world, and the spiritual forces of evil in the heavenly realms. So, we have an existence in that spirit world filled with good and bad angels, and God gives us armor so that we can win our part of the fight.

A final passage about the struggle going on in the spiritual realm is Revelation 12:7-12. Here, in the vision John has of what is happening in the realm where angels live, he sees "war in heaven." The good angels under Michael fight Satan and his angels over whether the risen Christ can take His place at the right hand of God. The good angels win, Christ takes His place, and Satan is now limited so that He can no longer accuse those who accept Jesus and have the blood of the Lamb working for them.

Today, that spirit realm still exists. Our souls are there, that part of us by which we remember, learn, and decide. And Satan and good angels and even God the Father, God the Son, and God the Holy Spirit are there. They are talking about us, and God is telling Satan that he cannot have us if we are living by His will. If, on the other hand, we give in to Satan's temptations, then we turn to his side and let Satan have us.

From these four passages, we learn that there is constant warfare in the spirit realm between good and evil. God made Adam and Eve with the power to choose—to eat or not to eat, to sin or not to sin. Satan talked them into sinning and so introduced sin into the world. They did not pass their guilt to us, but with sin now loose in the world, all who have followed them have also chosen to sin (Romans 3:23). Satan keeps on trying to win people to his side. There is war and it is over us. The comics picture it pretty well—a little angel on one shoulder and a little devil on the other, each trying to win our favor. We, however, make the choice—we cast the deciding vote. We know, of course, who wins in the end—God and the good angels and those who have accepted and followed Jesus. Strange that so many who know the final outcome do not choose to live so they live, and die on the winning side!

Angels, then, work on our behalf, but we don't understand much about how they do it. God sometimes sent angels appearing as human beings to help His people, and the writer of Hebrews suggests that such could still be the case (13:2). Angels do work behind the scenes for us and God may sometimes use them as He answers prayer.

From Daniel 10, let us recognize that God hears the prayers of the righteous, that He sometimes sends angels to answer prayers, and that God wants us to know His will and reveals it to us in various ways.

Sermon Thoughts from Daniel 10

What God Can Do: How God Answered Daniel's Prayer
1. God Knew What Daniel Prayed.
2. God Sent an Angel to Provide Daniel an Answer.
3. God Strengthened Daniel When He Was Afraid.
4. God Provided Daniel Information to Answer His Question.

Follow Daniel's Example (See above)
1. Daniel Lived so God Highly Esteemed Him.
2. Daniel Humbled Himself Before God.
3. Daniel Was Highly Dedicated to God.

God's Angels
1. **God's Angels Are Powerful.** Daniel's view of an angel is of one who is strong with a hard body, a face like lightning, eyes like flaming torches, and arms and legs strong as polished bronze.
2. **God's Angels Fight Bad Angels.** In several passages cited above, God's angels overpower the bad angels. God never allows Satan or his forces the final victory.
3. **God's Angels Serve Humans.** The angel who came to Daniel answered his prayer for more information. In Revelation 12, the good angels defeated Satan, thus allowing Christ to bring His sacrificial blood to God on our behalf. And, we

may sometimes entertain angels sent to help us without our recognizing who they are.

Satan Pursues Christians

There is indeed a war in the spirit realm over each one of us. Satan wants to take us with him to everlasting torment while God wants to take us with Him to eternal life. Satan works against us in three ways that are consistent with his nature.

1. **Satan Deceives.** John 8:44 says he is the father of lies. He lied to Jesus in Matthew 4 when he was tempting Him by twisting the meaning of a Scripture. He lies to us to tell us such things as "a little bit won't hurt," or "you can get as close to the edge as you can and it will be OK," and "you need to protect your own interests." We need to be alert to recognize the devil's lies to us so we do not fall for them. There may be people in your life through whom Satan will bring his lies to you.

2. **Satan Divides.** One of Satan's favorite tactics is to divide people. During the exodus, he kept dividing the people against Moses. During the time of the judges and kings, he divided God's people. When Jesus came, he got the Jews divided over Jesus with some accepting Him while the majority did not. He seeks to divide families and workers and churches. Resist the efforts of Satan to divide and be careful about people who do divisive things in your life.

3. **Satan Destroys.** In Revelation 9:11 he is called by names that mean "destroyer." God wants us to succeed in what we do, but we will not always have smooth sailing. Think of the story of Job, for example, when Job's entire family of children were killed at one time. Satan can use many different forces to work against us and we don't always know how he is operating. Just know that God wants us to succeed and will help us to reach that goal if we define success as God wants us to do.

CHAPTER 11

The Most Detailed Prophecy in the Bible

Daniel 11, written in 536 BC, tells of events that will happen between then and 166 BC. There is good agreement among most conservative scholars about the fulfillment of the first thirty-five verses of this chapter, and we shall deal with these in this chapter. As we walk through these predictions, you will see how detailed and how accurate they are. As we relate this story from history, the predictions the angel gave Daniel are placed in quotation marks so you can connect the prophecy with the history of what actually happened.

Daniel was told that "three more kings will arise in Persia, and then a fourth, who will be far richer than all the others" (11:2). Since Daniel was speaking in the days of Cyrus, the next three Persian leaders were Cambyses (530-522 BC), Gaumata (522 BC), who was an imposter, and then Darius I Hystaspis (522-486 BC). This king helped the Jews in rebuilding the temple in Jerusalem. The fourth king in the prophecy was Xerxes I (486-465 BC), who was "far richer than all the others." He was determined to conquer Greece as his father had failed to do. He marshalled a huge army, invaded Greece, and won great victories, but he suffered a major naval defeat when his larger ships were rammed and sunk by the more maneuverable, smaller ships from Greece in the Battle of Salamis. Following this loss, Xerxes returned to Persia and soon held a beauty contest. And the winner was—Esther.

So the four more kings had come as Daniel predicted. Skipping some lesser-known Persian kings, he then said that following the four he mentioned would come a "mighty king who will rule with great power" (11:3). His empire, however, "will be broken up and parceled out toward the four winds of heaven . . . . It will not go to his descendants" (11:4). These words, no doubt, predicted the "mighty king" Alexander the Great who exercised great power and, after his death at the age of 33, his kingdom was divided among four of his generals, not to his children.

At this point, the angel told Daniel about the relationships between two of the four generals and their successors. He called one of them the "king of the South" and the other the "king of the North" (11:5-6). They were so named because, standing in the land of the Jews, Seleucus I of Syria and those in his lineage would be to the north while Ptolemy I of Egypt and those in his lineage would be to the south. In verses 5-34, Daniel detailed how the kings of the North and kings of the South would deal with each other and often their movements toward each other would take them through the land of the Jews, which lay between them.

Verse 5 introduces us to Ptolemy I of Egypt, king of the South, and a prince or commander of his, who is Seleucus I. At the first he worked with Ptolemy, but later declared his independence from him. Just as the verse predicts, this commander would be "even stronger" than the first king, and Seleucus I reigned over much more territory than did Ptolemy. These two kings and their successors opposed each other, but in 252 BC, Ptolemy II hoped to improve matters by allowing his daughter, Bernice, to marry Antiochus II, thus "making an alliance." The problem with this arrangement, however, was that Antiochus II already had a wife, Laodice, whom he put away for Bernice. As the prophecy said of this plan, the new wife "will not retain her power, and will he [the husband] and his power will not last" (11:6). In retaliation for being put away, Laodice arranged for the poisoning of Antiochus II along with his Egyptian wife, Bernice, and their infant son. Then Laodice got her son, Seleucus II to be king, and he reigned from 246 to 225 BC. Speaking now of the murdered wife, "One from her family line will arise," a king of Egypt from the line of

Bernice, which would be Ptolemy III. He will "attack the forces of the king of the North [Seleucus II] . . . and be victorious" (11:7). He came to avenge the death of Bernice and was successful. Ptolemy III even captured the capital city of Antioch and killed Laodice.

As the angel continued to tell Daniel about future events, he said there would be continuing conflicts between the king of the North and the king of the South. He told, for example, about a king of the North, referring to Antiochus III, who would "assemble a multitude of great forces" (11:10) to attack Egypt, the realm of Ptolemy IV who responded and eventually defeated Antiochus III at the Battle of Raphia in 217 BC. Fifteen years later, however, Antiochus III "will muster another army, larger than the first" (11:13) and launch an attack on Egypt, ruled by Ptolemy V, conquering as far south as Gaza in 201 BC.

Next, some Jews, "the violent men among your own people" (11:14) would join the revolt against Ptolemy V to ally themselves with the Syrians under Antiochus III. He stayed for a time "in the Beautiful Land" of the Jews (11:16) and so, at that point, control over the Jews changed from the Ptolemys to the Seleucids. Later Antiochus III will give him a proposal of peace by giving Ptolemy V his daughter in marriage (11:17) hoping that move will give him more power in Egypt, but "his plans will not succeed" since his daughter sides with her husband rather than with her father (11:17). He will then "turn his attention to the coastlands and will take many of them," an accurate description of Antiochus's move to send a fleet of three hundred ships and to conquer islands along the coast of Asia Minor (11:18). The Romans, now a rising power in the east, send a "commander," however, who "put an end to his insolence" (11:18) by defeating him in 190 BC at Magnesia along the western edge of Asia Minor. He was forced to give his younger son, Antiochus IV, along with some others, as hostages to Rome. He returned to Syria and died in 187 BC, thus fulfilling the statement of verse 19 which says, "He

THE MOST DETAILED PROPHECY IN THE BIBLE

will stumble and fall to be seen no more."

Seleucus IV replaced his father as king and, as Daniel prophesied, "will send out a tax collector to maintain the royal splendor" (11:20). This statement was fulfilled when he sent Heliodorus to collect taxes. Before long, however, Seleucus IV died by assassination, "yet not in anger or in battle."

As we come to Daniel 11:21, the angel begins to reveal to Daniel what will happen in Israel when a "despicable person will arise." The actions of this person occupy at least through verse 34. Antiochus IV, called Epiphanes, became the next king over the Syrian Empire in 175 BC, and fulfilled to an amazing degree all of the details the angel revealed to Daniel. This same person was the "little horn" of Daniel 9:9, who was described there as taking away the daily sacrifice which would continue for "2,300 evenings and mornings and then the sanctuary will be reconsecrated" (8:14). Daniel 11, however, told of these events in much greater detail.

Antiochus IV was not the rightful heir to the throne, being the brother of the late king rather than the son, but, as Daniel prophesied, he took "the kingdom by intrigue" (11:21). After consolidating his position, he began to expand his kingdom by moving south. He would shatter "the prince of the covenant" thus taking control of the land of the Jews (11:22). Then he would move on into Egypt, taking authority away from Ptolemy VI and thus he will "achieve what his fathers never did." Because of his sense of greatness, he will "distribute plunder, loot, and wealth," and he even walked through the streets tossing handfuls of money and watching people scramble for it.

Antiochus IV and Ptolemy VI, then would negotiate together with "their hearts intent on evil," but their efforts would not succeed so Antiochus IV returned "to his own country with great wealth, but his heart will be set against the holy covenant. He will take action against it and then return to his own country" (11:28). As Antiochus went back home through the land of the

Jews, he entered the temple and took with him many of the sacred vessels.

After about two years, Antiochus IV decided to "invade the South again, but this time the outcome will be different from what it was before" (11:29). He went through Judea with his army and moved to Memphis in Egypt, which surrendered to him. Before he reached Alexandria, however, "ships of the western coastlands [Kittim] will come against him "(11:30). The Egyptians had appealed to Rome for help, and they responded with ships from the west. "Kittim" here is a reference to a city on the south coast of Cyprus, but in this passage stands for Roman ships coming from that direction. The Roman leader, Laenas, told Antiochus IV to leave Egypt immediately or face war with Rome. Antiochus asked for some time to consult his advisors, but the Roman leader drew a circle around him in the sand and said he must answer before crossing the circle. He, of course, had no choice but to agree, but was "disheartened" and, to vent his anger, he "showed favor to those who forsake at the holy covenant" (11:30). Thus, as he came back through Judea in 168 BC, he enslaved or killed eighty thousand people and robbed and "desecrated the sanctuary" (11:31). He also abolished "the regular sacrifice," and "set up the abomination that causes desolation" by erecting an altar to Zeus in the temple and sacrificing a pig on the altar (11:31). With "flattery" he deceived some Jews into working with him to try to Hellenize the Jews, but others "who know their God will firmly resist him" (11:32). "For a time" those who resist him "will fall by the sword or be burned or captured or plundered," but others will come to help (11:34). Thus, Daniel's words told of the beginning of the resistance to Antiochus IV, which would come through the rebellion led by the Maccabees.

So Daniel had prophesied about how kings came to power, how they married for political gain, how they fought and won or lost, how they died, how they treated the Jewish people and temple, and how the Jews would eventually have a successful rebellion against a king of the North. That is an accurate description of a period of time from 536 BC to 166 BC, and it was all told in advance of the time in which it happened.

No wonder those who do not believe in God or the accuracy of the Bible maintain that the book of Daniel was written about 166 BC by someone who already knew of the events described and could, therefore, write about it after the fact as if writing before it happened. As shown in the Appendix of this book, however, the evidence is strong that the book of Daniel was, indeed, written by Daniel and completed by about 536 BC.

Now we come to the passage from Daniel 11:36 through all of Daniel 12, the most difficult part of the book of Daniel to interpret. The discussion of these verses will be in Chapter 12.

In closing, let's note a few lessons we can learn about prayer from the prayer Daniel prayed from chapter 10 and the results of the prayer in chapter 11. (1) Daniel prayed about God's promises. Through Jeremiah, God promised to limit the Babylonian captivity to seventy years, and Daniel prayed that God would keep that promise. If there are promises of God you consider precious to you, pray about them and ask God to fulfill them. Maybe they are promises about His church or promises to take care of His people or promises to take us to be with Him. Praying the promises will inspire and encourage you, and God will fulfill His promises. (2) God does not always answer prayers immediately. Daniel prayed hard for twenty-one days and still found no answer coming. But he kept on praying. Though the answer to his prayer had begun when he started praying, he didn't know it. We may pray about something and think no answer is coming, but God may have started a way to fulfill the prayer which we won't know about for a while. God's answers to our prayers are not always immediate, but do not think your prayer is being ignored. (3) God answers every prayer. Sometimes the answer is *yes,* sometimes it is *no,* sometimes it is *wait,* and sometimes it is *take an alternative.* Daniel prayed for more understanding, and he received it (Daniel 10:12). The Bible gives many examples of answered prayer. David prayed for forgiveness and received it (Psalm 51:10-13). Hezekiah prayed for longer life and got it (Isaiah 38:3). Nehemiah prayed that Artaxerxes would help him rebuild the walls and he did (Nehemiah 1:4-2:9). The church prayed for strength to face persecution, and God granted it (Acts 4:23-31). Sometimes, however, God said *no* when some of His people prayed. Abraham prayed that Ishmael could be his heir (Genesis 17:8). Moses prayed that he could enter the Promised Land. (Deuteronomy 31:23-25). David prayed that his infant son would live (2 Samuel 12:16-18). And Elijah prayed for death (1 Kings 19:4). The Jews prayed through Old Testament times about the coming of the Messiah, but had to wait hundreds of years before that prayer was answered. Paul prayed that God would take away his thorn in the flesh, but God gave him an alternative—more grace (2 Corinthians 12:8). And Jesus prayed that the cup might pass from Him and God, while not granting that request, sent an angel to strengthen Him (Luke 22:3). Jesus prayed again that God would find another away, but then accepted that He must go through the torment and fulfilled His trial, persecution, crucifixion, and death.

So Daniel is a great example in prayer with passion and perseverance. And God shows that He wants us to pray and will respond when we pray according to His will.

Sermon Thoughts from Chapter 11

What God Can Do: God Uses Agents to Attain His Ends

1. **God Used Angels to Attain His Ends.** God sent an angel to tell Daniel about the future, and when the angel was delayed by an angel of Satan, God sent Gabriel to get him through to Daniel. This allowed the lower-ranking angel to reveal the future to Daniel.

2. **God Used Daniel to Attain His Ends.** Daniel submitted

himself to God many times and in many ways and thus, made himself a vessel for God's use. He used him to reveal dreams to Nebuchadnezzar, to advise him as his prime minister, to show God's power to protect a faithful servant from lions, to tell Belshazzar of his coming doom, and to reveal the future by recording his visions.

3. **God Used Pagan Kings to Attain His Ends.** God could use pagan kings to do His will without their even knowing He was using them. Nebuchadnezzar didn't know God was using him to fulfill His word to the Jews that, because of their continued idolatry, he would send them to Babylon. Cyrus didn't know God was using him to carry out His will to bring the Jews back from captivity. Xerxes didn't know God was using His decree to kill the Jews as a means of bringing about a great triumph for the Jews through Esther. Antiochus IV did all he could to wipe out the Jewish religion, but his actions brought on the Maccabean rebellion, which provided a period of freedom for the Jews for a hundred years and laid groundwork for the coming of Christ. The Romans didn't know God had predicted through Daniel (2:44; 7:13-14) that their Empire would exist at the time when He would establish a kingdom. The Jews and the Romans didn't know that by sending Jesus to the cross they were playing a part in God's great drama for saving those who would accept Jesus. And the Romans didn't know that in destroying the city of Jerusalem, they were fulfilling God's promise to the Jews that, because of their rejection of Christ, He would bring their city to ruin (9:26).

How God Responds to Prayer (See above)

DANIEL: WHAT GOD CAN DO
CHART 8

Daniel 11:2-35

Prophecy	Fulfillment
3 kings in Persia: 4th richer	Spoken in reign of Cyrus. Next four are Cambyses, Smerdis, Darius Hystapes, and Xerxes.
4th shall stir up all against Greece.	Xerxes attacked Greece in 480 BC and won some victories, but lost the decisive Battle of Salamis.
Mighty king stands up to rule.	Alexander the Great of Greece.
Kingdom broken; divided in four directions, not to posterity.	When Alexander died, kingdom went to four generals and not to his posterity.
King of South will be strong.	Ptolemy I of Egypt.
Prince strong above him.	Seleucus I became stronger and over more territory.
Two joined by marriage of daughter of K of S to K of N.	In 252 BC, Bernice, daughter of Ptolemy II married Antiochus II. He put away first wife, Laodice.
She shall not retain strength nor he stand.	Laodice poisoned Antiochus II and Bernice and her son. Seleucus II became king.
K of S will enter land of K of N.	Ptolemy III attacked Seleucus II and was victorious.
K of N will attack K of S but not win the victory.	Antiochus III attacked Ptolemy IV and regained some territory, but did not win in Egypt.
K of N will attack K of S but K of S shall win.	Antiochus III again attacked Egypt and conquered all of Palestine but Ptolemy IV beat him at Raphia.
K of N returns with larger army.	Antiochus III comes again and wins at Panion.
K of N gives daughter to K of S but ploy fails.	Daughter sides with husband, K of S, and so K of N gains no advantage by this political marriage.
K of N turns to isles but a prince shall bring him down.	Antiochus III conquered some islands off the coast of Asia but the Romans defeat him (Magnesium-190 BC).
K of N to send tax collector.	Seleucus IV sends Heoiodonus for temple money.
Comes a contemptable person who gains throne by flattery.	Antiochus IV not true heir; wins kingdom by intrigue. (This one is the same as the little horn of chapter 8).
Shall break prince of covenant.	He shall depose Onias II, high priest; puts in his own.
Will do what fathers didn't.	Takes even lower Egypt.
K of S and K of N lie to each other but not succeed.	Did not keep another claimant from becoming king.
K of N returns. Stops sacrifices.	Antiochus IV returned through Judea.
K of N comes south again but ships of Kittim shall oppose.	Moves into Egypt but Roman ships bring commander.
Profanes temple. Take away sacrifice. Set up abominations.	Who says he must leave Egypt. Turns vengeance on Jews and Jerusalem. Stops sacrifices. Offers swine sacrifice. Set up abominations.
Some will resist.	Judas Maccabeas starts rebellion. Succeed.

CHAPTER 12

The Prophecy Comes to a "Time of the End"

So far, we have studied different prophecies of Daniel, which have carried us through basically the same time sequence several times. The chart below summarizes these predictions and reviewing this information will help us as we begin to look at the last part of the last prophecy revealed to Daniel.

Kingdoms	Daniel 2	Daniel 7	Daniel 8	Daniel 9	Daniel 10-12
Babylon	Head of Gold	Lion with wings			
Medes/ Persians	Chest and arms of silver	Bear eating 3 ribs	Ram with 2 horns, last is greater	70 sevens start with decree to build. 7 sevens	4th king of Persia is rich, stirs up Greece
Greeks	Belly and thighs of bronze	Leopard with wings	Goat— one horn which breaks and four arise. From one comes a little horn	62 sevens	Mighty king arises, kingdom to four others. Kings of North and South fight over Judea. King of fierce countenance
Romans	Legs of iron/ feet of iron/ clay	Beast with iron teeth		70th seven starts with coming of anointed one. Prince destroys city.	

THE PROPHECY COMES TO A TIME OF THE END

Kingdoms	Daniel 2	Daniel 7	Daniel 8	Daniel 9	Daniel 10-12
Kingdom of God	Stone cut out—destroys statue	Son of Man comes to receive kingdom		Anointed one ends sin and brings in righteousness	

From this chart, we get the breadth and scope of the five prophecies in Daniel. They all predict earthly kingdoms that will play a part in the future of the Jewish nation. They also predict the coming of Christ as the ultimate king. These prophecies tell of a nation that would teach the Jews to stay away from idols, of another nation that will allow them to return to rebuild their temple and reestablish observance of the law. They would go through a time of anguish under a king of fierce countenance but resistance would arise and eventually they would win a time of freedom. Finally, there would come a divine kingdom over which the Messiah would reign when the seventieth seven arrived.

The final verses of Daniel 11 through chapter 12 are much more difficult to understand than are the earlier prophecies, and no one can be certain of the precise interpretation. We must not, however, allow this to take away from the marvelous accuracy with which Daniel predicted coming events in previous portions of his book. So now we move to study the last part of chapter 11 and chapter 12.

Daniel 11:36 says, "The king will do as he pleases. He will exalt and magnify himself above every god and will say unheard-of things against the God of gods. He will be successful until the time of wrath is completed, for what has been determined must take place." There are primarily three different interpretations offered for who this "king" is, and we shall take a brief look at all three of these options before drawing our final conclusions about the book of Daniel.

Some would say that this passage refers to "the antichrist"

who shall come at the beginning of seven years of tribulation just before the Lord's second coming. They say there will be a moment of "rapture" when all dead Christians will be raised in their new bodies and all living Christians will be changed into their new bodies and these two groups will then be taken into heaven to be with Christ. During the seven following years, the antichrist, or some say two antichrists, will rebuild the Jewish temple in Jerusalem with the offering of the Jewish sacrifices resumed, and then there will be war over Israel climaxing in the Battle of Armageddon. As this battle reaches its climax with more than 300,000,000 soldiers fighting in the land of Israel, Jesus will return with the raptured saints, put down the fighting, and begin a thousand-year reign on earth. According to this view, the good Old Testament saints will be raised at that time to participate in this kingdom along with those converted to Christ during the seven years of tribulation.

So, let's examine this possibility. Does the Bible teach that there will be one or two antichrists that will come seven years before the return of Jesus to take actions to plunge the world into a final battle? Does this passage in Daniel, along with other Bible passages, teach this plan for the end of the world? Since this is such a widely held theory, we shall take a rather extensive look at this view.

1. Let's first examine all of the verses in the Bible which use the word *antichrist*. There are only four of them, all in the epistles of John. Surely the verses that use the word should give us the best view of how Scripture intends us to understand this term. First John 2:18 says, "as you have heard that the antichrist is coming, even now many antichrists have come." Then 1 John 2:22 says, "Who is the liar? It is the man who denies that Jesus is the Christ. Such a man is the antichrist—he denies the Father and the Son." In 1 John 4:3, the writer continues, "but every spirit that does not acknowledge Jesus is not from God. This is

the spirit of the antichrist, which you have heard is coming and even now is already in the world." And finally, 2 John 7 says "Many deceivers, who do not acknowledge Jesus Christ as coming in the flesh, have gone out into the world. Any such person is the deceiver and the antichrist."

So let's ask some questions. How many antichrists will there be? John says "many." When will they start to come? In his own day, the first century. John says "even now many antichrists have come." John, tell us what makes a person to be an antichrist? He "denies that Jesus is the Christ." "He denies the Father and the Son."

When we study the only four verses in the Bible that use the term *antichrist*, we learn that an antichrist is one who denies that Jesus is the Christ, that there will be many antichrists. and that many such people existed even in the first century. This information does not match what we hear so often that there will be one or two antichrists and that these one or two will come shortly before Jesus returns. Since the prefix *anti* means "against," the term *antichrist* simply means one who is "against Christ." Since the first century, there have always been those who have denied Christ, and so there have always been many antichrists.

Though those who contend that there will be one or two antichrists who will come near the end of the world look to some other passages we will not examine here, if the four verses in the Bible that actually use the word do not support their view, then other passages they say present the concept will have another explanation.

2. Allow me to offer another thought or two about this theory, and then we will return to the book of Daniel. According to the "antichrist" scenario, living and dead Christians will be "raptured" into heaven seven years before Jesus returns, and then the antichrist will appear. This timetable, then, says that the antichrist comes seven years before Jesus'

second coming. That scenario would mean that we can know precisely when Jesus will return—just count down seven years after the rapture. But the Bible says often that Jesus' second coming will be "like a thief in the night." (See Matthew 24:43; Luke 12:39; 1 Thessalonians 5:2; 2 Peter 3:10.) If, however, we had a seven-year tip off, then we would know exactly when Jesus is returning.[1]

3. First Thessalonians 4:13-17 is the primary passage on which those who support the "rapture" theory base their belief. It says that "the dead in Christ shall rise first. After that, we who are still alive and are left will be caught up together with them in the clouds to meet the Lord in the air. And so we will be with the Lord forever." The expression from this passage they use is that "the dead in Christ shall rise first" and so, say those holding this theory, the Christian dead will be raised before others are raised. But does the passage say that? The dead in Christ will be raised before something, but before what? The passage says the dead will be raised in their new bodies before the living are changed into their new bodies. This passage does not teach that there will be more than one resurrection. It does not say that some are raised before others are raised. It says, rather, that the dead are raised in their new bodies before the living will be changed into their new bodies. Thus, the dead are at no disadvantage compared with the living when Christ returns. So, not more than one resurrection taught here—or anywhere else.

In fact, John 5:28-29 says "a time is coming when all who are in their graves will hear his voice and come out," and the verse then names both the good and the bad. So—all raised at once. And in John 6:39, 40, 44, and 54, Jesus repeats the

---

[1] I have written a book about the doctrines of the "rapture," rebuilding the temple, antichrists, the Battle of Armageddon, and the thousand-year reign. It is called *Like a Thief in the Night* and may be purchased through 21st Century Christian in Nashville, Tennessee or online at 21stcc.com.

THE PROPHECY COMES TO A TIME OF THE END

same message—that His followers, the righteous, will be "raised on the last day." The "rapture-antichrist" theory says Christ's followers will be raised before a seven-year tribulation and a thousand-year reign—a total of 367,555 days before the last day. So Jesus says that all are raised at the same time and that will be on the last day.

This brief look at the idea that there will be a resurrection of the Christian dead along with a transformation of living Christians called the "rapture," followed by the coming of an antichrist who will rebuild the Jewish temple and plunge the world into a huge war over Israel does not match a number of passages of Scripture. Although this study does not review all of the passages to which people holding this theory turn, we have examined all four of the passages that use the word *antichrist* and these should be our primary guide. Surely these passages are the best place to learn what the Bible means when it speaks of *antichrist*.

One more quick thought. The "rapture" theory says that the Christian dead will go to heaven and after seven years come back to earth to live for a thousand years in a good but still imperfect world. Do you believe it would be a good plan to go to heaven where all is perfect for seven years and then have to come back to earth where all would not be perfect to live for a thousand years? God has a better plan for us than this.

In view of these thoughts, then, we can reject the interpretation of Daniel 11 that says it speaks of a coming antichrist who not only did not come during any of the time periods of which Daniel is speaking, but who, even 2,500 years later still has not come.

So we have discussed option one, that Daniel 11:36 begins a discussion of an antichrist and have rejected that possibility. Here is option two. Many fine scholars hold that at this point in Daniel, the picture leaves Antiochus IV to turn to a discussion of the coming Roman Empire. After all, they say, in three of the earlier prophecies, the picture has moved forward to Roman times—the legs of iron, the beast with iron teeth, and the seventieth week. Wouldn't it be likely that this final prophecy in the book would also move to that time period? And some of the descriptions certainly could fit the Roman Empire such as (1) "He will invade many countries and sweep through them like a flood," and (2) "He will invade the Beautiful Land," and (3) "Egypt will not escape." So, the Roman view has much to recommend it and it could be the meaning of this part of Daniel.

Let's, however, take a look at a third possibility which may fit the description even a little bit better. Since these final words of the angel are not as specific about historical events as the earlier part of Daniel 11, we cannot tie them to history as easily as we did those earlier verses. And, since 11:36-45 mention again the king of the South and the king of the North, one would think that the activities of Egypt versus Syria are still in view. And the focus of the prophecy is still about "the Beautiful Land," which lies between them. This section could, then, be viewed as a general summation of the experience of the Jews with Antiochus IV in less specific terms than those used in earlier verses. History does not confirm that Antiochus IV made an additional attack on Egypt, although new discoveries often illuminate something we did not know had occurred. The best approach, then, could be to think of these verses as a broad summation of what has been previously described.

Another important question here is the expression in 11:40 about "the time of the end." That this statement would take us from Antiochus IV, who is under consideration at least through verse 36, and move all the way to the final end of time is certainly unlikely. Without more details, that conclusion would certainly be doubtful. Scripture sometimes uses a phrase like "time of the end" to refer to the end of the time period under discussion

THE PROPHECY COMES TO A TIME OF THE END

rather than pointing to the final end of time when Jesus returns.

Continuing to explore the view that the angel is summing up the prophecy and giving Daniel a view of things to come for the Jewish nation, Daniel 12:1 says, "At that time Michael, the great prince who protects your people, will arise." Since Michael helped get a lesser ranking angel through to Daniel (10:21), and since he preserved the body of Moses from Satan (Jude 9), he appears especially to work on behalf of the Jews.

The early part of Daniel 12 continues to tell that sometime in the future, the Jews would be under distress, but at that time, those whose names are written in the book will be delivered (12:1). As early as Exodus 32:33, God has been keeping a list of those who are His, and Psalm 28 also mentions such a list. The list here, then, could fit any time period for God's keeping a list of His people and one of the clear options for the meaning of this verse would be the list of those God would return from Babylonian captivity. That concept seems to fit well here because the next expression says that "Multitudes who sleep in the dust of the earth will awake: some to everlasting life, others to shame and everlasting contempt" (12:2). Of course this at first sounds like a reference to the final resurrection of the dead, but that interpretation would involve quite a time leap from speaking of Antiochus IV through at least 11:35 and either of him or the Romans through the end of chapter 11.

Another possibility would be that this reference to those who come out of the dust would have a similar meaning to that found in Ezekiel 37:12-13 where Ezekiel, who lived at the same time as Daniel, saw the dry bones coming back to life. This vision is a reference to the nation of the Jews returning to their land following the Babylonian captivity. Such an understanding of this passage in Daniel would also fit well the time frame of these verses, because Daniel received the prophecy near to the time of the return from Babylon. The faithful returned while others, who might have become disobedient, would be those who would suffer contempt. Verse 12:3 says, "Those who are wise will shine like the brightness of the heavens, and those who lead many to righteousness, like the stars forever and ever." The return of the Jews to their own land would take away shame from their God and would allow them again to be in the land He promised them. Thus, they would shine for Him.

Then the angel told Daniel to "roll up and seal the words of the scroll until the time of the end" (12:4). The angel does not want Daniel immediately to publish the prophecy he has given. When the time was right, however, people would read the words to learn what God had said and to know of His ability to predict accurately future events. We don't know, of course, just when the prophecy of Daniel was released, but since it was included in the Septuagint, it was likely known before 200 BC when the Septuagint translation was begun.

There is one final scene in the book of Daniel, still another encounter with angels. There is a wide variety of views on the meaning of this portion, and no one can know for sure just how to understand it. In 12:5-13, Daniel sees three angels. One angel is standing with Daniel on one side of the Tigris River while another angel is on the opposite side. A third angel, the one who has been providing the revelation since Daniel 10 began and who is clothed with linen, is positioned above the waters of the river. The one nearest to Daniel asks the one above the river, "How long will it be before these astonishing things are fulfilled?" To this question, the one above the river holds up his hands and "swears by him who lives forever, saying, 'It will be for a time, times and half a time. When the power of the holy people has been finally broken, all these things will be completed'" (12:7). Expressions like "time, times, and half a time" are used in scripture in a figurative way to designate an unspecified period of time. If the word *time* is used for "year," then this expression could mean three and a half years or 1,260 days, but these words could still represent a figurative length of time. The meaning here is

THE PROPHECY COMES TO A TIME OF THE END

also that this last prophecy will take a while to be fulfilled, but it will end with the holy people being broken. The Jews were certainly strongly oppressed during the days of Antiochus IV, so it could have reference to being broken then. Some see this as a prediction of the eventual destruction of Jerusalem, which Daniel prophesied in chapter 9, and with that came the breaking of the holy people.

Complicating the process of understanding the meaning of the "time, times and half a time," are the next verses. "From the time that the daily sacrifice is abolished and the abomination that causes desolation is set up, there will be 1,290 days. Blessed is the one who waits for and reaches the end of the 1,335 days" (12:11-12). Some connect these periods with Antiochus IV's stoppage of the sacrifices in 168 BC by suggesting that he desecrated the temple for 1,260 days but that it was another 30 days before the Jewish sacrifices actually were re-started, making 1,290 days. Then, by 1,335 days Antiochus IV had been killed. Others connect these times with the army coming to surround Jerusalem in 70 AD and eventually to destroy it.

Though these times remain a mystery, we should give special attention to the last verse of Daniel 12 when the angel tells Daniel to go his way "till the end. You will rest, and then at the end of the days you will rise to receive your allotted inheritance" (12:13). Daniel would have been in his mid-eighties by the time of this prophecy and so had not many years left. This likelihood, the angel says, should not be discouraging but rather Daniel had much to which to look forward. He will rest and then will rise to receive his inheritance.

What a great way to end the book of Daniel! A promise that though he will come to the end of this life, he will rise to something much better. All of us should keep our eyes on that distant goal. Even when problems arise and tragedy strikes, we should know that the difficulties of this life will in no way mar our ultimate inheritance when we rise to inherit a new life.

So, we conclude one of the most beautiful books in the Bible. It tells the story of a teenager who is carried from Judah, totally separated from his family, his culture, and his people, and taken into a land where virtually everyone else is worshiping pagan idols and engaging in many sinful practices. The chances of his remaining faithful to God under those circumstances would seem remote indeed. Yet, at the risk of his life, he refuses to eat food that would defile him, according to the Law of Moses. He finishes a three-year program of studies to become an advisor to the most powerful man on earth and immediately demonstrates that, through his God, he is wiser than all the other advisors by telling the king what he had dreamed and what it meant.

Still, as a very young man, he is promoted to the second-highest position in the realm where he serves his king admirably, even accurately interpreting for him an unfavorable dream that predicts the king will live for a time like an animal. When the king actually suffers such an event and then is restored, Daniel's faithfulness leads the king to honor Daniel and his God—truly an example of how Daniel let his light shine even in a dark place.

When other kings have arisen and Daniel is no longer prominent in the government, God sends a handwritten note to Belshazzar, inscribed on the wall of a beautiful banquet hall while a great feast is going on. No one can understand the message, and Daniel is called to interpret. He tells the king that his kingdom is lost, and he will die that night. The Medes/Persians are already using their strategy of changing the flow of the Euphrates River to conquer Babylon, and Daniel's words are fulfilled exactly.

As the new kingdom comes to power, Daniel is again given a high position—one of three who rule over the 120 governors. Before long, as a man now in his eighties, Daniel has so distinguished himself that the Persian king plans to give him second place in the Empire. Others are jealous but can find nothing he has ever done wrong so they trick the king into saying that no one can ask anything of anyone but him for thirty days, believing that Daniel will continue his practice of praying three times a day with his window open toward Jerusalem. And, they are right. Nothing can prevent him from his prayers and for punishment, he is thrown into a den of lions. Because God wants to demonstrate His power and because He wants to reward Daniel for his faithfulness, God shuts the mouths of the lions and Daniel is unharmed.

What a striking life! The teenage boy who is carried away from family and other believers in God into a totally idolatrous culture, is faithful in every aspect of his life. And this young lad eventually serves as the prime minister of two of the great world empires and does it with total faithfulness to God.

God also uses Daniel as the agent through whom He delivers amazingly accurate predictions about coming centuries, and through these prophecies and their publication prior to their fulfillment, strengthens our faith even today.

Sermon Thoughts from Daniel 12

What God Can Do: God and His People

1. **God protects His people** (12:1). Even in this life, God cares for His people and works on many ways in their behalf.

2. **God reveals His word** (12:4). God has given Daniel prophecies about the future and in so doing, has shown that He can foresee the future and can reveal it in advance. God also reveals to all how He wants them to live.

3. **God raises the righteous** (12:13). There will be an end to the world at which time God will raise Daniel and all those who have loved his appearing. Although the wicked will also be raised, the righteous will be raised to receive a wonderful inheritance.

The Challenge for God's People (12:3)

1. **The wise will shine like the brightness of the heavens.** God's people should be lights for the world. Jesus gives this charge in Matthew 5:14-16 when He calls on us to "let your light shine." Whether teens in their schools, or those on their jobs, or the elderly facing the end of life, we should all find ways to show the beauty of living as God would have us to live.

2. **Those who lead many to righteousness (will shine) like the stars forever.** Nothing makes Christ happier than for us to confess His name to others (Matthew 10:32). Second Corinthians 5:16-21 tells us that we are Christ's ambassadors to reach the lost.

God's Promise to His People (12:13)

1. **Live faithfully.** Go your way till the end (of your life). Do not wander away. Do not let the coming end of life cause you to wander. In whatever way you can, continue to serve.

2. **Then will come rest.** The time of death for the faithful Christian is not a defeat but a rest. Though the final victory awaits, there will be peace and rest. Many Christians who suffer at the end of their days enjoy the peace of the sleep of death.

3. **Finally, the faithful rise to receive an inheritance.** Jesus has gone to prepare a place for us and what a place He would be able to prepare (John 14:6). In Revelation 20, the New Jerusalem comes down into John's view so he can get a glimpse of what the new heaven and earth will be like—and his description of it in figurative terms gives us all great hope for this final inheritance.

THE PROPHECY COMES TO A TIME OF THE END

CHART 9

Summary of Prophecies

Kingdoms	Daniel 2	Daniel 7	Daniel 8	Daniel 9	Daniel 10-12
Babylon					
Medes/Persians					
Greeks					
Romans					
Kingdom of God					

Completed Charts

CHART 2

Picture	Daniel's Interpretation	Further Interpretation
Head of Gold	Thou art the head of gold.	Nebuchadnezzar's Babylonian Empire was powerful and rich.
Breast and Arms of Silver	After Nebuchadnezzar, another kingdom, inferior.	Medo-Perisan Empire conquered the Babylonians in 539 BC. Not as opulent.
Belly and Thighs of Bronze	Third kingdom which shall rule over the earth.	Next the Grecian Empire under Alexander the Great took the Persians in 331 BC.
Legs of Iron Feet/Iron and Clay	Fourth kingdom, strong as iron, will break in pieces and crush all before it.	Romans used iron for spears and they crushed all before them.
	Feet and toes of iron mixed with clay—a divided kingdom. Partly strong and partly broken.	After its strong period, Rome gradually grew weaker. Other powers (Goths, Visigoths, Huns, Vandals) shall attack. Vassal kings will rebel.
Stone Cut out Without Hands	In the days of those kings (of the last of these empires), God shall set up a kingdom which shall never be destroyed.	In the days of the Roman Empire, Christ is born, lives, and establishes His kingdom (Mark 1:15; 9:1).
Smote the Image	God's kingdom shall triumph over the others and will continue while they fail. It will have a part in their overthrow.	This kingdom is still here long after the others are gone and the church eventually played a part in the fall of Rome.
Stone Became a Mountain		God's kingdom is world-wide and remains through time.

CHART 4

Picture	Daniel's Interpretation	Further Interpretation
Lion coming out of the sea	A king who shall arise out of the earth (v. 17)	Nebuchadnezzar. Palace was guarded by winged lions.
Eagles wings		
Wings plucked off. Then stands as a man.		Nebuchadnezzar was humbled in his time of mental illness. Recovered and was restored.
Bear coming out of the sea.)	A king who shall arise out of the earth (v. 17)	Cyrus and the Medo-Persian Empire
Raised up on one side.		Persian side higher than Mede side
Three ribs		Slower than a lion but more powerful Eating nations as it goes forth
Devour much		Larger territory than Babylon.
Leopard coming of the sea.		Alexander and Grecian Empire
Four wings		Fast moving and ferocious Kingdom divided to four generals
Four heads		Larger territory than Persians
Dominion given		
Fourth beast out of the sea	A king who shall arise out of the earth	Roman Empire
Terrible, strong	Devour whole earth	Roman army conquered everywhere
Great iron teeth		Romans took more territory than others
10 horns	10 kings shall arise	Could be first ten emperors.
Little horn comes. Eyes of a man	Another king, put down 3 kings.(v. 24)	Roman Emperor Domitian, 11th but 8th if not count 3 who ruled a short time
Speaks great things.	Speaks against Most High	Domitian set himself as god. Demanded worship. Images of himself.
Made war with saints. Eventually fails. Saints possess kingdom.	Wear out saints for times, and half a time. Eventually saints take his kingdom.	Domitian killed Christians who would not worship his image. Rev. 12:14 uses same length of time (1,260 days) as time of intense persecution. Rev. 20, saints reign in victory over the beast. Kingdom of Christ continues. Romans gone.
Throne placed for Ancient of Days.		
Throne on wheels		Majestic. Present everywhere.
One like Son of Man comes to take kingdom.	Saints of Most High receive eternal kingdom	Christ called himself "son of man" (Matt. 26:64). Peter called Him both Lord and Christ (Acts 2:36).

CHART 6

The Ram and the Goat From a Study of Daniel 8

Picture	Daniel's Interpretation	Further Interpretation

Ram
  Two horns.
  Higher came up last
  Pushing west.
	Kings of Media and Persia	Empire of Medes and Persians.
		
		Greater Persian side came up last. Came from east; went west, north, south

Goat
  Came from west
  Didn't touch ground
  Notable horn
  Smote ram.
  Trampled
  before river.
  Magnified himself.
  Great horn broken.
  4 horns came up.
	King of Greece (v. 21)	Greece came from west toward Persia
		Moved very rapidly
		
		Alexander the Great Conquered Persia in 331 BC. Decisive battle was at Granicus River
		
		Very powerful and proud. Died in 323 at age 33. Kingdom divided among 4 generals.
		Cassander—Macedonia;
		Lysimachus—Greece;
		Ptolemy-Egypt;
		Seleucus—Asia

From one horn comes a "little horn"—glorious land.	King of fierce countenance (v. 23)	Descendants of Ptolemy and Seleucus fight with Judea between them. From Seleucus comes Antiochus IV (175-164 BC) who oppresses the Jews.
Cast down stars Took away the continual burnt offering. 2300 days. Then cleansed	Shall destroy holy people Shall magnify himself. Stand against the prince	Kills many Jews. Take away temple sacrifices. Offers swine on the altar. Desecration of temple lasted about 2300 days—171 to 164 BC. Then cleansed.

CHART 10

Summary of Prophecies

Kingdoms	Daniel 2	Daniel 7	Daniel 8	Daniel 9	Daniel 10-12
Babylon	Head of gold	Lion with wings			
Medes/ Persians	Chest and arms of silver	Bear eating ribs	Ram with 2 horns, last is greater	70 sevens start with decree to build. 7 sevens	4th king of Persia is rich, stirs up Greece.
Greeks	Belly and thighs of bronze	Leopard with wings	Goat— one horn which breaks and four arise. From one comes a little horn	62 sevens	Mighty king arises, kingdom to 4 others. Kings of North and South fight over Judea. King of fierce countenance
Romans	Legs of iron/feet of iron/ clay	Beast with iron teeth		70th seven starts with coming of anointed one. Prince destroys city	
Kingdom of God	Stone cut out— destroys statue	Son of Man comes to receive kingdom		Anointed one ends sin and brings in righteousness	

Appendix

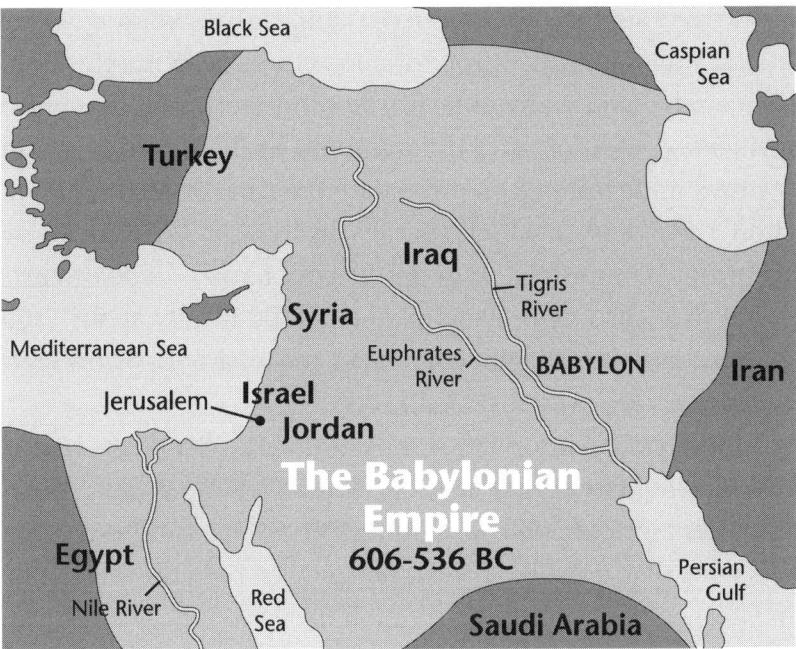

For those who have a special interest in more details about the world situation in Daniel's time and in the question of Daniel's authorship, this Appendix provides additional information. Much of Daniel involves major nations from about 600 to 166 B.C., so a clear picture of the world during that time can be useful. And since the interpretation of Daniel turns on whether it was written by the person whose story it tells or by someone about four hundred years later who was writing in the name of such a person, we must also study the question of who wrote Daniel and when.

APPENDIX

Both the city and the nation of Babylon are important in studying Daniel. Even before his time, this area of the world played an important part in the life of many Bible characters. The story of the tower of Babel (sounds nearly like Babylon) took place some years after the flood and describes people of that area as quite proficient in building large structures. About 1930 BC, Abraham was called from Ur of the Chaldees. Like Babylon, Ur was located on the Euphrates River, being to the southeast of Babylon as the river approaches the Persian Gulf. Ur had buildings three or four stories high, the people manufactured beautiful furniture and jewelry, and many of its features indicate a well-developed civilization in Abraham's time. A room in the British Museum features finds from Ur that pre-date the time of Abraham and show the extent to which that civilization had developed by his time. Hammurabi, who produced a famous code of laws, established the city of Babylon about 1700 BC. By about 1300 BC, the Assyrian Empire controlled the area of Babylon with occasional revolts by the Chaldeans.

This historical information tells us that the city where Daniel lived during the events of his book was a famous place in an important location on the Euphrates River. By his time, the city was more than a thousand years old and had been the capital city of major empires, and the civilization there was highly developed.

Shortly before the story of Daniel begins, some important new events take place in Babylon. The Assyrian king dies and Nebopolassar, a Chaldean, declares himself king of the eastern part of the Assyrian empire with Babylon as his capital. His son, Nebuchadnezzar, leads armies to the west to secure as much territory as he can, destroying the remaining Assyrian Empire in 612 BC, and moving on south to conquer Jerusalem about 605 BC.

Following this conquest of Jerusalem, Nebuchadnezzar sets up his own vassal Jewish king, Jehoikim, and takes young men from some of the noble families to Babylon to train them for service in his kingdom. Among these are Daniel, Hannaiah,

Mishael, and Azariah. About that same time, Nebopolassar dies and Nebuchadnezzar, his son, becomes the king. In 602 BC, Jehoikim, King of Judah, rebels and in 597, Nebuchadnezzar comes against Jerusalem again, this time re-conquering it and taking more captives to Babylon including Ezekiel who, thus, is in Babylon when he writes his prophetic book.

In 586 BC, Jewish puppet king Zedekiah rebels against the Babylonians and by this time, Nebuchadnezzar has had enough. He brings his armies against the city, captures it, destroys Solomon's beautiful temple, which has stood there for more than three hundred years, and burns the rest of the city. This time, most of the people of Judah are taken to Babylon as captives.

Nebuchadnezzar even conquers much of Egypt and spreads his kingdom into most of modern-day Turkey. He was truly the most important and most feared leader of his day.

Nebuchadnezzar also adds many new buildings to the city of Babylon so that it becomes the most beautiful city in the world. Among the things he builds there is the hanging gardens, which are noted as one of the seven wonders of the ancient world.

Following Nebuchadnezzar come other kings of Babylon, including Nabonidus who becomes king in 555 BC. Because he travels often around his empire to keep order among his people and to worship his god in a special place, he appoints his son, Belshazzar, to be king in the city of Babylon itself. By 539 BC, however, a new power has arisen to the east of Babylon—the union of two groups, the Medes and the Persians. This growing empire first defeats an army of the soldiers from Nabonidus and then comes against the city of Babylon itself. Because of the high protective walls and the storehouses of food, those in Babylon think they are invincible, but the attacking force has a great strategy. Since the Euphrates River runs under the wall of the city, they divert the flow so the river's water level will go down far enough for soldiers to march under the wall of the city to conquer it without opposition.

APPENDIX

The Medes and Persians then make Babylon their capital city and from there control even more territory than had the Babylonians. In 331 BC, however, a force from the west confronts the Medes and Persons. Alexander the Great has mobilized sufficient forces to defeat them and to take control of the vast territory the Medes and Persians had possessed. Soon, however, Alexander dies at the age of thirty-three and his empire is divided among four of his generals who now constitute different kingdoms rather than a single, unified one. Soon, still another major power begins to grow from even further west—from Rome. And by the first century before Christ, they rule more territory than any of these preceding empires.

In studying Daniel, one should keep in mind this general progression of world empires—the Babylonians, the Medes/Persians, the Greeks, the Romans. This progress plays a major role in the study of Daniel.

Now to the question of authorship

Two possibilities typically are offered. The first is that a man named Daniel, who lived around 600 BC and is the main character in the story, is the one who had the prophetic revelations and wrote them down during his lifetime. The other option is that some unknown person who lived during the second century before Christ wrote the book using the name of Daniel to encourage those involved in the revolt against Antiochus, which was called the Maccabean Rebellion.

If Daniel actually wrote the book, then his prophecies of events to come in the following six hundred years were written long before they happened and prove that God can foresee the future and can reveal it to those who can write it down well before the events actually take place. If, on the other hand, the book was written after the events took place, then what appears as prophecies in the book of Daniel are only recorded after the fact and, thus, are not examples of God's revealing the future.

So the view one takes about the date of the writing of Daniel is extremely important not only in interpreting the meaning of the book, but also in how one views the Bible. If Daniel, indeed, wrote the book, then it is one of the best examples the Bible's foretelling future events with great accuracy. So, to which conclusion does the evidence lead—to actual prophecies of the future or to an impersonator writing of events in a prophetic style when the events have already happened?

First let's look at the view that holds that the book was written about 165 BC. One of the arguments given for this view is that the book of Daniel tells accurately of events that happened after 600 BC, but since they assume it is impossible to predict the future accurately, the book must have been written after the events it describes. Those holding this view say, further, that Daniel contains three Greek words naming musical instruments (3:5, 7, 10, and 15). Since Alexander had not spread the Greek language to the Middle East by 600 BC, the argument goes, the book must have been written after the time of his conquests, and thus after 330 BC. Another argument is that Daniel misspoke about Nebuchadnezzar whom he called "king" when he came against Jerusalem in 606 BC since he did not actually become king until the following year when his father died. Another inaccuracy, according to this view, is that Daniel misses how long Jehoikim has been ruling by calling the fourth year of his rule his third. Though these are not all of the things those who hold the late date would mention, they are a good sampling of them.

First, let's examine these arguments for the date of about 165 BC, and then we will give arguments on the other side. One should not start with the assumption that there is no such thing as predictive prophecy. First, we should examine the evidence for Daniel's early date and then make that decision. As to the three Greek words Daniel uses for musical instruments, it should be noted that since the Greek language was around long before the days of Alexander and, since people traveled and traded back and

APPENDIX

forth among the nations, it would not have been unusual for some Greek words to work their way into another language before that language became universal. As to calling Nebuchadnezzar "king" before he actually became king, we need only to look at common expressions today. One might say, for example, that President Bush was born in Texas, though he was not president when he was born. We often use a person's later title when speaking of him before he gained that title. Regarding the years of a king's reign, the Babylonians counted one's reign with a "zero" year as the first, and "one" as the second. So, Daniel, writing in Babylon, used the Babylonian method of counting. Thus, these arguments against the early date for Daniel are not strong at all.

Now let's consider reasons for regarding the book of Daniel as having been written near the 600 BC time and then ask which view appears more likely, 165 BC or 600 BC.

1. Ezekiel, writing from Babylon during the lifetime of Daniel, mentions him as a figure of importance who was wise and righteous (Ezekiel 14:14, 20; 28:3), thus indicating that such a person was well-known during the Babylonian exile.

2. Of special significance is the fact that Jesus refers to Daniel as "the prophet" and applies one of his prophecies about the destruction of Jerusalem (Matthew 24:15). This prophecy of Daniel, Jesus said, had not yet been fulfilled but would be soon. Thus Jesus regarded Daniel as a prophet, and as able accurately to predict future events. This means that, according to Jesus, Daniel wrote a prophecy in earlier times, which had still not been fulfilled by 30 AD, but which would be fulfilled in the destruction of Jerusalem, which happened in 70 AD. So, Jesus tells us to believe in the predictive prophecy of Daniel. Incidentally, Jesus also frequently called Himself "the son of man," a phrase which Daniel used of the coming king (Daniel 7:13-14).

3. Josephus says that the Old Testament canon was closed

in the time of Ezra, Nehemiah, and Malachi and that no more books were added after that time. He also reports that Jewish leaders showed Alexander the Great the book of Daniel and told him it had prophesied about his coming (Antiquities, XI, viii, 5).

4. The book of Daniel is included in the Septuagint. About 200 BC, Jewish scholars began translating the Hebrew Old Testament into Greek, since by that time Greek was almost a universal language. We do not know exactly the date when the book of Daniel was translated to be included in the Septuagint, but a book not even written until 165 BC would surely not have been considered as a part of the sacred Scriptures to be included in such a translation.

5. Among the Dead Sea scrolls at least seventeen fragments of the book of Daniel have been identified. These fragments are dated about 165 BC, but the scholars copying at Qumran would certainly not have included among the books of importance for them to copy a book not even written until that year.

6. The book of Daniel shows familiarity with details of history that could not have been known by someone who lived in 165 BC. He knew of Nebuchadnezzar's building activities and about punishments, dress, banquets, customs, and laws. A person living over four hundred years later and without historical information only available later could not have included such information.

7. Any knowledge about Belshazzar, crown-prince and co-ruler of Babylon along with his father Nabonidus, disappeared by the time of Herodotus (c. 450 BC) and was not discovered until the Nabonidus Chronicle and certain Cuneiform tablets were found in 1882. The book of Daniel, however, not only mentions Belshazzar but gives details of his death along with the fall of Babylon. Since no one from about

APPENDIX

500 BC until 1882 AD had any knowledge of Belshazzar, it is clear that a person living in 165 BC could not have written about him.

8. Details in the book of Daniel are in complete agreement with the Cyrus Cylinder, discovered in 1879, which says that Cyrus conquered Babylon "sparing any calamity" and that he allowed Jewish captives in Babylon to return to their home country.

The book of Daniel cannot be the work of an honest, well-meaning forger. Either it is a prophecy or it is a fraud. The attempt by critics who wish to avoid the power of Daniel's accurate predictions of future world events by assigning his book a date "after the events took place" falls when subjected to the tests of history and archaeology. The book was written when and where it claims and does speak accurately of events several hundred years in the future.

Study Guide

LESSON 1

Historical Setting for Daniel

(*Use to Begin Chapter 1 and the Appendix*)

1. Provide students a notebook in which to keep materials from this course. One of the sheets you should provide in the notebook is a sheet on which students can record practical lessons they learn from the book of Daniel as they move through the lessons.

2. Ask what class members remember about the book of Daniel.

3. Share with the class the objectives for this course and encourage them to do the assignments suggested in the lesson to help them reach the objectives.

4. Using the chronology and some passages of Scripture, review the historical background for the book of Daniel including the fall of the Kingdom of Israel for idolatry, the rise of Babylon, the first conquest of Jerusalem to Nebuchadnezzar and what he took with him to Babylon (people and temple utensils), the second conquest, and the third conquest and destruction. Use a map if possible to show the geography involved.

5. Review from the Appendix what you consider to be the most useful information for your class about the factors to show that Daniel wrote the book of Daniel during his lifetime rather than the book's being written about 166 BC.

6. Assign class to read Daniel 1.

LESSON 2

The Decision About the Food

(Use to Review Chapter 1)

1. Remind students about writing on the sheet provided in their notebook the practical lessons they find for themselves in the book of Daniel.
2. Using the information in Chapter 1 and with students in the class having their Bibles open to Daniel 1, ask the class questions about the circumstances Daniel and his three friends faced when they were taken to Babylon and put in the training program.
3. Questions for discussion:
    a. Why did Daniel refuse the king's food? (It did not fit the dietary provisions of the Law of Moses; it had been offered to idols and partaking would make him appear to approve of the idols.)
    b. What personal qualities does Daniel show in the refusal to eat the food? (Courage, respect for his captors, leadership, honesty, determination.)
    c. Who appears to be in control of the events? (See verses 2 and 17. What does this suggest to us?)
    d. What situations might we face today that would be similar? (Think of people of all ages and in a variety of circumstances.) How should we deal with these?
4. Assign the class to read Daniel 2.

LESSON 3

The King's Dream

(*Use Chapter 2*)

1. Review the story of Daniel 1.
2. With their Bibles open to Daniel 2, under your questions, let the class put together the story of this event up to the point where Daniel tells the dream and its interpretation.
3. As you come to the dream, either use the board or a PowerPoint image of the statue from the Internet to give the class the image seen in the dream.
4. Using Chart 1 provided, let the class complete columns two and three with your help as needed. The completed chart is also provided for your use (Chart 2).
5. Ask what practical lessons the students can draw for themselves from Chapter 2.
6. Assign the reading of Daniel 3.

LESSON 4

Decision in the Plain of Dura
(*Use Chapter 3*)

1. Review the image of Chapter 2.
2. Tell of Nebuchadnezzar's building activities—hanging gardens, palaces, Ishtar gates.
3. Through questions to the class, tell the story of Chapter 3.
4. What qualities do Shadrach, Meshach, and Abednego demonstrate, which we should use as an example?
5. Let the class tell of situations in their lives when they are faced with similar circumstances of being like those around us or standing up for our faith.
6. Assign the reading of Daniel 4.

LESSON 5

The King's Mental Illness

(*Use Chapter 4*)

1. Review the previous lesson about the Decision in the Plain of Dura.
2. Note that all of Daniel 4 is a document written entirely by King Nebuchadnezzar to his empire—the only long passage in the Bible written by a pagan king.
3. With their Bibles open to Daniel 4, let the class help tell the story of (1) the king's dream, (2) the interpretation of the dream, (3) the king's insanity, and (4) the king's confession.
4. What other kings does the Bible suggest that God brought down in some way?

    (Pharaoh with the plagues, the King of Assyria in Jonah's day, Belshazzar in Daniel 5, Herod Agrippa I in Acts 12:20-23.)
5. What practical lessons do we learn from this story about Nebuchadnezzar? Remind students to write these practical lessons on the sheet provided in their notebook.
6. Assign the reading of Daniel 5.

LESSON 6

Handwriting on the Wall

(Use Chapter 5 in the book)

1. Review the last lesson about Nebuchadnezzar's mental illness in Daniel 4.

2. Review the historical background for this lesson. The Babylonians have been in power since they defeated the Assyrians in 612 BC. They have a great and beautiful capital city in Babylon, which has high, wide walls for protection. King Nabonidus spends most of his time away from the city and has left his son, Belshazzar, as king in Babylon. Discuss how information about Belshazzar came to light. The Babylonians know that the Medes and Persians have joined forces and want to defeat them, but they feel secure in their fortified city.

3. Review the story of Daniel 5.

    a. The feast—1-4. Be sure to discuss the use of the utensils from the temple.

    b. The handwriting—5-16. Include discussion of the "third position."

    c. The interpretation—17-28.

    d. The result—29-31.

4. Share the historical information about how the Persians took the city.

5. Let the class read some verses from Jeremiah 50 and 51 and tell how they connect with the fall of Babylon.

6. What practical applications can we make from this story?

LESSON 7

The Lions' Den

(*Use Chapter 6 in the Book*)

1. Review the previous lesson from Daniel 6.
2. Set up the historical situation. The Medes and Persians have captured the city of Babylon and taken over the Babylonian Empire in 539 BC. They have placed Daniel, who is now in mid-eighties, as a high-ranking official in their empire. Show a map of their empire.
3. With the class members having their Bibles open to Daniel 6, ask questions to review the story of the chapter.

   a. The Plot—verses 1-9.

   b. The Response—verses 10-11. Why was prayer so important to Daniel? Why did he not pray in secret? What statement was he making by continuing to pray as he always had?

   c. The Judgment—verses 12-18.

   d. The Rescue—verses 19-28. Why did God rescue Daniel? Does he rescue all His children who are in trouble? Does God rescue people today? Why some and not others? God needs people in all kinds of circumstances who show how their faith in God sustains in those circumstances—even bad ones. Many early Christians went to their deaths at the mouths of lions. See 2 Timothy 4:17.

4. What practical lessons can we learn from this lesson? What circumstances for us would be like what Daniel faced?
5. Assign the reading of Daniel 7.

LESSON 8

The Four Beasts

(*Use Chapter 7 in the Book*)

1. With Daniel 7, we enter the second half of the book, the part which contains four prophecies Daniel received about future events relating to the Jews.
2. By asking questions as much as possible, help the students complete Chart 3 for Daniel 7. Chart 4 has the completed Chart 3 for the teacher's use.
3. Using Chart 5, compare this prophecy with the one in Daniel 2. Chart 6 has the completed Chart 5. Ask the students to keep Chart 5 so they can continue to complete it as the class moves through additional prophecies.
4. What practical lessons so we learn from this study?

LESSON 9

The Ram and the Goat

(*Use Chapter 8 in the Book*)

1. Review Lesson 8. Note the similarities between the prophecies in Daniel 2 and Daniel 7.
2. Using questions, let the class help complete Chart 5.
3. Note the differences between the "little horn" of Daniel 7 and the "little horn" of Daniel 8.
4. Fill in additional information in Chart 5. (Chart 6 is for the teacher's use.)
5. Ask the class for practical lessons to learn from Daniel 8. (Use Chapter 8 in the book for ideas.)

LESSON 10

Prophecy of Seventy Sevens

(Use Chapter 9 in the Book)

1. Review the previous lesson over Daniel 8.
2. Using questions, let the class develop the story and prophecy of the chapter.
   a. The Occasion—verses 1 and 2. 1st year of Darius the Mede would be 539 BC. Daniel has been reading Jeremiah 25:9-11.
   b. The Prayer—verses 3-19.

   What are outward signs of Daniel's sincerity?

   With what does Daniel begin his prayer? (Praise.)

   What does Daniel do on behalf of his people? (Confesses sins.)

   What does Daniel say God was right to do? (Send the Jews into captivity.)

   What does Daniel ask God to do? (Keep His promise to restore the sanctuary and the city.)

   How does Daniel reason with God about doing this? (It is for God's glory.)
   c. The Response—verses 20-23.
   d. The Prophecy—verses 24-27. Use Chart 9 to help the students understand this prophecy. Emphasize verse 27 to show that the Anointed will confirm a covenant (Jeremiah 31:31) and will put an end to the Jewish sacrificial system (Hebrews 8:6-13; 10:4).
3. Assign Daniel 10 for class to read before the next meeting.

LESSONS 11, 12, AND 13

The Coming Struggle Over the Land of the Jews

(*Use Chapters 10, 11, and 12 in the Book*)

1. Daniel receives word about the future in 536 BC. At this time he would be in his mid-eighties and would be serving Cyrus, the Persian monarch. After receiving a message about the future, he prays to know more about it, but it is three weeks before he receives an answer.

2. Discuss the work of angels using the information in Chapter 10 of the book as a basis for questions and answers. Determine how much time to spend on this topic based on the amount of time you have to finish the remainder of Daniel.

3. Using Chart 10, guide the students through the prophecy and fulfillment. Emphasize two things in this discussion: (1) that the prophecy was written hundreds of years before the events took place and (2) that the predictions are very specific.

4. Review Daniel 11:36 through the end of Daniel 12. Emphasize 12:13.

5. Save as much of the last class period as possible to discuss the practical lessons students have written in their notebooks about what they have learned from Daniel. Help them to make specific applications. For example, if someone says, "I can apply this at work," then say, "Describe a specific situation in which you might use this lesson at work." If he/she says, "When we are in a meeting." Then say, "Tell me how the conversation might go in the meeting when you would use this lesson."

Bibliography

Butler, Paul T. *Daniel.* Bible Study Textbook Series. Joplin, Missouri: College Press, 1970.

Hailey, Homer. *A Commentary on Daniel.* Las Vegas: Nevada Publications, 2001.

Leupold, H. C. *Exposition of Daniel.* Grand Rapids, Baker Book House, 1969.

McGuiggan, Jim. *The Book of Daniel.* Looking Into the Bible Series. Lubbock, Texas: Montex Publishing Co., 1978.

Myers, Edward P; Pryor, Neale T.; Rechtin, David R. *Daniel, Truth for Today Commentary.* Searcy, Arkansas, Resource Publications, 2012.

North, Stafford. *Like a Thief in the Night.* Nashville: 21st Century Christian, 2004.

North, Stafford. *Unlocking Revelation.* Nashville: 21st Century Christian, 2003.

Robinson, Thomas. *The Preacher's Complete Homiletic Commentary on the Book of Daniel.* New York: Funk & Wagnalls, n.d.

Wilson, Robert Dick. *Studies in the Book of Daniel.* Grand Rapids: Baker Book House, 1979.